T0224880

Beyond Accessibility Compliance

Building the Next Generation of Inclusive Products

Sukriti Chadha

Forewords by
Mike Shebanek, Head of Accessibility at Meta
Larry Goldberg, Founder of Teach Access and XR Access

Apress®

Beyond Accessibility Compliance: Building the Next Generation of Inclusive Products

Sukriti Chadha
Lookout Mountain, TN, USA

ISBN-13 (pbk): 978-1-4842-7947-2 ISBN-13 (electronic): 978-1-4842-7948-9
https://doi.org/10.1007/978-1-4842-7948-9

Copyright © 2023 by Sukriti Chadha

Managing Director, Apress Media LLC: Welmoed Spahr
Acquisitions Editor: James Robinson-Prior
Development Editor: James Markham
Coordinating Editor: Jessica Vakili

Distributed to the book trade worldwide by Springer Science+Business Media New York, 233 Spring Street, 6th Floor, New York, NY 10013. Phone 1-800-SPRINGER, fax (201) 348-4505, e-mail orders-ny@springer-sbm.com, or visit www.springeronline.com. Apress Media, LLC is a California LLC and the sole member (owner) is Springer Science + Business Media Finance Inc (SSBM Finance Inc). SSBM Finance Inc is a **Delaware** corporation.

For information on translations, please e-mail booktranslations@springernature.com; for reprint, paperback, or audio rights, please e-mail bookpermissions@springernature.com.

Apress titles may be purchased in bulk for academic, corporate, or promotional use. eBook versions and licenses are also available for most titles. For more information, reference our Print and eBook Bulk Sales web page at http://www.apress.com/bulk-sales.

Any source code or other supplementary material referenced by the author in this book is available to readers on the Github repository: https://github.com/Apress/Beyond-Accessibility-Compliance. For more detailed information, please visit http://www.apress.com/source-code.

Printed on acid-free paper

Table of Contents

About the Author

Sukriti Chadha is a mobile developer turned product manager who currently works at Spotify as the accessibility product manager across all platforms. Her current focus is fan monetization, after working on scalable mobile infrastructure to enable reliable shipping of Spotify's mobile apps to its over 450 million users globally.

Sukriti started as a mobile developer at Yahoo Finance in 2016. Her father's vision loss in one of his eyes due to complications from diabetes inspired her to work with accessibility stalwarts, and to patent, launch, and open source technology that allows people with visual impairments to use charts and interpret data using music, haptics, and voice synthesis. She also developed a system for haptic navigation for people with hearing impairments.

Sukriti is an invited expert at W3C with WCAG (Web Content Accessibility Guidelines) and the Mobile Accessibility Task Force. WCAG is the industry working group that sets the guidelines that are the ISO standard for accessibility and the basis for the Americans with Disabilities Act (ADA). She also serves on the Mozilla Product Advisory Board, which hundreds of thousands of developers reference.

She is regularly invited to speak at conferences, including CSUN (the most prominent annual accessibility conference), A Future Date Conference, Product-Led Festival, Mobile Growth by Branch.io, and App Promotion Summit. Her project on automated mobile testing for accessibility won the Product-Led Alliance award for the most impactful project and the Product Developer of the Year American Business Award (Stevie Award).

Sukriti is also an active member of Teach Access, a collaboration of accessibility experts, industry leaders, and academics with companies such as Google, Microsoft, Facebook, and Walmart to further understand inclusion and accessibility among high-school and college students. As part of this initiative, she regularly collaborates with university professors who have expressed a desire to have a book like this as the foundation for their design and CS courses.

Sukriti has a Bachelor of Science degree in Electrical Engineering and a certificate in Finance from Princeton University. She is an instrument-rated pilot and a certified yoga instructor.

LinkedIn profile: www.linkedin.com/in/sukriti-chadha/

About the Technical Reviewer

Ashley Firth is Global Head of Front-End Development and Accessibility at award-winning energy supplier Octopus Energy. Since the company's formation, he has worked with customers to understand their needs and use new technology to make an online experience and an energy supplier as inclusive as possible. Ashley and Octopus Energy have won numerous customer and digital experience awards for their products. His book *Practical Web Inclusion and Accessibility*, also published by Apress, reached number one in the Amazon technology charts. The book guides people through a broad range of access needs and the barriers users often face and provides practical advice on how your sites can help rather than hinder. Ashley was shortlisted for the Young Energy Professional of the Year award for customer service, spoke at the Festival of Marketing on the importance of web accessibility, and was part of eConsultancy's first-ever Neurodiversity report. Apart from writing and public speaking, he acts as a consultant to government bodies and private companies to help them improve their approach to accessibility. You can find him on Twitter and Instagram at @MrFirthy.

Foreword by Mike Shebanek, Meta

There are certain people you meet that you know instantly are going to do extraordinary things. Sukriti Chadha is one of those people, and this book is one of those things.

Unknown to me when we first met, Sukriti was only beginning her journey into accessibility. At that time, we were working together on an invention that would soon be patented; a way for people with vision loss to understand and use charts and graphs. It's now included in the Yahoo Finance app and available to anyone with a smartphone – and that was just the first accessibility project she took on. Since then, Sukriti has amassed a world of knowledge about how to make software products and programs accessible, and thankfully for all of us, she is making that knowledge available to everyone.

In this book, Sukriti will present both a macro- and micro-view of accessibility, from broad concepts like "what is disability" and "how do we make a business case" to Project Management, test tools, researching user needs, the nuances of coding for accessibility in mobile app development, and strategies for creating an effective accessibility program. In so doing, Sukriti is able to share many fascinating real-world case studies because she's "been there" and "done that." She is also able to offer a unique perspective, having been both a software engineer and a product manager, who has learned the hard way, employing her skills and craftsmanship in the crucible of the tech industry. What she is able to share isn't found in an undergraduate degree or even a postgraduate education, and it is rarely codified on such a grand scale in a single book (electronic or otherwise). No doubt this is why Sukriti chose to take on such a project and make it available. It's a resource she and everyone working in the field of accessibility wish they had access to sooner.

If you already have some familiarity with accessibility and need or want to dive deeper, then you'll find this book invaluable. If your journey is just beginning, you have no idea how lucky you are to be starting here. (Perhaps you should stop reading for a moment and go buy a lottery ticket!) Either way, this is a resource you will come to value dearly because the knowledge and experience it contains is hard to find and even harder won.

Mike Shebanek, Head of Accessibility at Meta; former Head of Accessibility at Apple, Yahoo, and Verizon Media

Foreword by Larry Goldberg, XR Access

"To work in the field of accessible technology, one must be a diehard optimist."

In the long history of the drive to make the digital technology of our daily lives fully inclusive for everyone, what strikes me are not the frequent gaps, bugs, and barriers experienced by people with disabilities. No, it's the many successes that prove over and over again that, yes, you can build it right; yes, smart, capable designers and developers who are dedicated to excellence can in fact create stuff that works for everyone. That #BornAccessible is more than just an inspiring meme.

Sukriti Chadha is one of the people who justify my optimism. From the first time we met at Yahoo, it was evident that here was a person – a very young one at that – who was going to advance the field, who was going to make good, accessible things happen. With this book, Sukriti generously shares her knowledge with anyone and everyone who wants to rise above the at-times bug-riddled world of MVPs and bad betas. Step by step, thoroughly and clearly, this book says, "yes, you can." To Sukriti, I say "thank you." To everyone else I say, "no more excuses, read this book."

Larry Goldberg, former Head of Accessibility at Yahoo; Accessible Media and Technology consultant; Founder of XRAccess and Teach Access

Note 1:

    Thoughts, recommendations, and best practices in this book are purely the author's and not representative of current or former employers, institutions, or organizations.

Note 2:

    The author will donate all royalties from this book to the Vista Center for the Blind.[1]

[1] https://vistacenter.org/

Acknowledgments

To my dad, because of whom I first became interested in accessibility. To my mother and brother for their unflinching support and encouragement. To my extended family and friends, who taught me the beauty of embracing differences.

To Ahsan Barkatullah, for constantly reminding me how far I have left to go. To Philip Probasco, without whose partnership and confidence I would be lost. To Susan and Ben Probasco for embodying selfless love.

To Mike Shebanek, for his brilliance, generosity, and leadership. To Larry Goldberg and Jean-Baptiste Quéru for giving me the opportunity to learn from the best.

To my mentors, teachers, and coworkers for their support and guidance. Special thanks to Yatin Kaushal, Gary Moulton, Darren Burton, David Grandinetti, Katie Quehl, and the Yahoo accessibility team for their contributions to the Audio/Haptic Charts initiative. To Mark Pavlyukovskyy, Poshak Agrawal, Ashley Dubois, and Rahul Subramaniam for their friendship and astute advice. To Dani Devasa for his thorough feedback, and to Audrey O'Clair for believing in me.

Last but not least, thank you to my editors and the Apress team and to Alice Maglio for the illustrations.

Introduction

In the last few decades, technology has changed our lives in profound ways, determining how we perceive and interact with the world around us. While we have made enormous strides in bringing cutting-edge software products to mass markets as an industry, we have left behind people with disabilities. The annual research conducted by WebAim in 2021 reported that over 97% of the world's top 1,000,000 websites fail even the basic automated audits.[1]

Why is it that we can build self-driving cars and launch satellites into space and yet not figure out how to make everyday products work for people with disabilities at the most basic level?

I first learned of accessibility as a discipline while working as an Android developer at Yahoo Finance. During that time, my dad lost vision in one of his eyes due to diabetic retinopathy. That was when I started exploring how people with visual impairments use their smartphones. The first initiative I led was making financial market charts more accessible using alternate modes including tones (audio) and haptics (touch) to convey primarily visual data. This feature is covered in more detail in Chapter 1.

Over the next few years, I worked extensively on building accessible mobile applications as a developer. After transitioning into product management, I worked on including and prioritizing these efforts in product roadmaps at companies (Yahoo and Spotify) that serve hundreds of millions of users. One of the most surprising early facts I learned was that the WHO estimates one in seven people worldwide lives with some form of disability. That is about 15% of the world's population, which is over one billion people.[2]

Today's millennial workforce is driven by purpose and making an impact.[3] The opportunity to serve more than one billion underserved people seems like an obvious one. Why is accessibility still an afterthought? Clearly, there is a disconnect between

---

[1] https://webaim.org/projects/million/

[2] www.who.int/health-topics/disability

[3] https://sustainablebrands.com/read/organizational-change/what-matters-most-to-millennials-millennials-want-to-matter

the motivation for impacting people's lives and the resulting products that leave out an astonishing 15% of people worldwide.

One of the main reasons for this is that people in the best position to drive change are either not aware of the gravity of the problem space or they have not considered the meaning of *impact* holistically. These are people involved in the product development lifecycle including, but not limited to, product managers, engineers, marketers, designers, and data scientists.

Impact = People reached x Impact on each person

What is missing from the equation is the opportunity cost of excluding potential customers and employees by not being inclusive, and the disproportionate potential impact on this underserved market segment.

Impact = (People reached x Impact on each person) - (People excluded x Impact on each person)

Most literature on accessibility centers around design. While the design is an important component, the lack of accessibility generally is a prioritization issue. Designers are not even engaged, nor engineers given the task if accessibility isn't a priority for the company or product team. Increased litigation[4] and advocacy are helping shift this conversation into the mainstream, but to translate this momentum into results, we need to change our thinking to incorporate a more nuanced, 360-degree view of the product development lifecycle. The lessons and framework in this book will help you do just that.

---

[4]https://blog.usablenet.com/a-record-breaking-year-for-ada-digital-accessibility-lawsuits

CHAPTER 1

The Billion People Question

In the introduction, we identified prioritization as the main reason for the state of accessibility in today's technology products. The second biggest challenge after prioritization is know-how. Undergraduate technology programs, software training programs, boot camps, and eventually technology companies often do not include accessibility as part of core training for product teams. So even when accessibility becomes a priority, teams might not have the necessary knowledge to build accessible products or resolve issues in existing products. We will address both of these challenges in the book. Before we dive into the specifics of these problems, and their solutions, let's cover some basics.

What Is a Disability?

First, it's important to understand what we mean by the term disability. Disability is defined as a physical or mental condition that limits a person's movements, senses, or activities.[1] The organization that develops the guidelines for digital accessibility, the World Wide Web Consortium (W3C), considers disabilities ranging from visual, auditory, physical, speech, cognitive, language, learning, to neurological.

---

[1] www.lexico.com/definition/Disability

© Sukriti Chadha 2023
S. Chadha, *Beyond Accessibility Compliance*, https://doi.org/10.1007/978-1-4842-7948-9_1

Note that this definition does not consider whether the disability is temporary, momentary, or permanent. A person focused on driving a car is effectively disabled from looking at their smartphone while driving. Similarly, someone without a speech impediment, who speaks to a voice assistant with an accent that the device does not understand, is effectively speech impaired for that interaction.

People also perform movements and activities in response to or because of their environment. It is not necessarily a disability that puts them at a disadvantage but how the world around them is built that prevents them from effectively engaging with it. The WHO (World Health Organization) changed its definition of a disability from a "personal attribute" as it was described in 1980, to include personal and environmental factors.[2]

This broader understanding of disability helps builders of software products empathize with users who do have permanent disabilities, understand they have the power to change the environment around people with disabilities to make it more friendly, and as a result, build better products for everyone. This definition is also consistent with the social model[3] (as opposed to the medical model) of disability, which considers social and environmental factors as limitations instead of a person's medical condition.

What Is Accessibility? What Is Inclusion? What Is the Difference?

In short, accessibility is the quality of being easy to approach, reach, enter, speak with, use, or understand,[4] for everyone including people with disabilities. Automatic sliding doors are more accessible to someone with muscular dystrophy than a push handle door. A Kindle is more accessible to someone with glaucoma than a small print book.

The term accessibility is often confused with regulatory compliance or meeting standards set by third parties. The goal of compliance is to ensure that providers meet a *minimum* set of requirements which do not guarantee a product is usable.

---

[2] www.who.int/health-topics/disability#tab=tab_1
[3] https://disabilityinpublichealth.org/1-1/
[4] www.dictionary.com/browse/accessibility

Compliance may be enough *legally*, but industry-leading products such as the iPhone are not built only to meet minimum requirements. They are loved because they are inclusive, exceed minimum regulatory requirements, and are delightful to use. They exceed customer expectations.

Consider the difference between the two ramps shown in Figures 1-1 and 1-2, both compliant, and yet so very different.[5]

Figure 1-1. *Picture of a 60-foot-long ramp that looks like a maze and visually takes up the entire front of the house, with unnecessary turns leading up from a street to the door of a house*

---

[5]www.theguardian.com/commentisfree/2014/feb/14/60-metre-wheelchair-ramp-britain-great

Figure 1-2. *A ramp leading from street level to the door of a house, with side rails and one turn*[6]

Fun fact: Accessibility is also referred to as *a11y* in the tech industry. It is pronounced A-Eleven-Y. The 11 stands for the number of characters between the *a* and the *y*.

Power in Numbers

Fifteen percent of the world's population is a significant number. Business leaders and policymakers are coming to understand that it simply makes good business sense for products to be accessible (Figure 1-3). For software businesses, being inaccessible means they are limiting their reach and failing to retain existing customers who with age might develop disabilities.

---

[6]www.rehabmart.com/post/the-ultimate-wheelchair-ramp-buying-guide-how-to-choose-the-best

Figure 1-3. *User funnel with 15% hollowed out. Building products that 15% of the population can't easily use limits the potential reach of the product from the outset*

Why do 97% of the top one million websites still have basic accessibility issues?

The one billion number alone does not help us during the design, engineering, and testing phases of product development because:

1. There are functional needs of users with different types of disabilities beyond those of the general population.

2. Sometimes these needs are at odds with each other.

3. Users may have multiple disabilities that require unique design and engineering solutions.

4. Sometimes, teams view accessibility as an optimization instead of a core value. They are okay trading off what is perceived as additional work to build accessible products, as long as they can show enough overall growth.

One example of this is the need for large tap targets on touch-screen devices. While these will benefit people with motor impairments, partial vision, and cognitive disabilities, they also limit the amount of content that can be displayed on a given screen size. So, for example, users with low vision might need to scroll or scroll more often to access all of the content. In Chapter 7, we will discuss personalization, multimodal interactions, and emerging technologies as potential solutions.

Disability methods, thresholds, and reporting vary widely by country, which is why available global statistics are only approximations. To get a relative sense of the scale and a high-level breakdown of the types of disabilities, we can look at the Center for Disease Control's (CDC)[7] statistics for the United States in Figure 1-4.

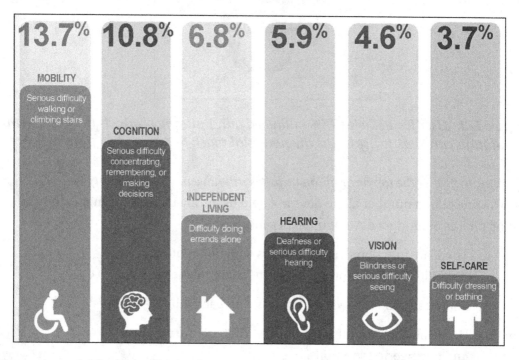

Figure 1-4. *Of the 61 million adults in the United States who live with a disability, the following categories affect the most people – 13.7% mobility, 10.8% cognition, 6.8% independent living, 5.9% hearing, 4.6% vision, and 3.7% self-care*

---

[7] www.cdc.gov/ncbddd/disabilityandhealth/infographic-disability-impacts-all.html

Summing up the numbers in Figure 1-4 exceeds 15% of the US population. This is because many people have multiple disabilities, and simply summing up people represented in each of the categories would lead to double-counting.

Note that globally, the percentage of people with disabilities is much higher given the differences in nutrition levels, healthcare, social services, etc. According to the World Health Organization, 80% of people with disabilities live in developing countries.[8]

The Rich History of Innovation Inspired by People with Disabilities

When we build products to address the needs of people with disabilities, we almost always end up building better products for everyone. Several mainstream technologies we use today are the result of innovations that were originally built for people with disabilities.

People with disabilities are often some of the most creative problem solvers because they constantly have to navigate a world where large parts simply weren't built with them in mind.

Curb cut is a classic example. Initially meant to help wheelchair users, pedestrians constantly find themselves in situations where they are grateful these ramps exist. Some other notable innovations used by everyone but inspired by people with disabilities are

> - Typewriter, 1808 – The first typewriter was built by Pellegrino Turri to help a blind friend write legibly.[9]

> - IBM, 1886 – Herman Hollerith, who had a cognitive processing disability, implemented the idea of using punch cards to transport data from the 1890 census. He later founded the Tabulating Machine Company. In 1924, it became known as IBM.[10]

> - Audiobooks, 1934 – The Readphon Talking Book was invented.[11] These were early audiobooks that for copyright reasons could only be used by visually impaired users.

---

[8] www.globalcitizen.org/en/content/disability-in-the-developing-world/
[9] https://nfb.org/images/nfb/publications/bm/bm00/bm0002/bm000205.htm
[10] www.ibm.com/ibm/history/ibm100/us/en/icons/tabulator/
[11] www.accessiblesociety.org/topics/technology/eleccurbcut.htm

➢ Transistor, 1948 – John Bardeed, William Shockley, and Walter Brattain at Bell Labs invented the transistor to create more reliable, smaller, cheaper, more efficient hearing aids. They won the 1956 Nobel Prize for Physics.[12]

➢ Email, 1972 – Vinton Cerf, who had a hearing impairment and was married to a deaf woman, developed host-level protocols for ARPANET. He communicated with his wife through the computer using text – the precursor to email.[13]

➢ Keyboards, 1988 – Retail registers began to use picture-based keyboards, originally created to help those that couldn't speak be able to use a synthesizer to talk.

➢ Captions, 1998 – Synchronized Accessible Media Interchange (SAMI) was released to allow simplified ability to caption and audio describe videos.[14] In a 2019 survey, it was found that 69% of people watch videos with the sound off in public places and that 80% of people who use captions do not have a hearing impairment.[15]

➢ Kitchen tools, 1990 – Sam Farber founded OXO Good Grips[16] kitchen tools when he saw his wife with arthritis having trouble using cooking tools.

➢ OCR, 1976 and computer-generated speech – Ray Kurzweil invented the first optical character recognition machine[17] that read computer-generated speech for the blind. Today, our cars, home assistants such as Amazon Echo are based on the same technology.

---

[12] www.academia.edu/6058944/Hearing_Aids_and_the_History_of_Electronics_Miniaturization_2011_

[13] www.hearingloss.org/wp-content/uploads/Cerf_Interview_MayJune2009_HLM.pdf?pdf=2009-hlm-mj-bchertok

[14] www.w3.org/WAI/sami.html

[15] www.streamingmedia.com/Articles/ReadArticle.aspx?ArticleID=131860

[16] www.oxo.com/blog/behind-the-scenes/behind-design-oxos-iconic-good-grips-handles/

[17] www.historyofinformation.com/detail.php?entryid=1170

If this isn't enough to motivate investment in accessibility, maybe this excerpt from a 2018 Accenture report will be

> *The U.S. Department of Labor's Office of Disability Employment Policy categorizes persons with disabilities as the third-largest market segment in the U.S., after Hispanics and African-Americans. The discretionary income for working-age persons with disabilities is $21 billion—greater than that of the African-American and Hispanic segments combined.*[18]

Policy and Regulations

This section will explore some of the existing policy frameworks that are widely used by technology companies and regulators as benchmarks for assessing digital accessibility. While the nuances and implementation vary, the spirit of these regulations and guidelines is the same – to establish a baseline for accessibility.

In a landmark decision in October 2019, the Supreme Court of the United States ruled in favor of a blind user who sued Domino's after being unable to order a pizza from their website.[19] The defense lawyers argued that ADA only applied to brick-and-mortar retail stores but not online stores. This was a win for disability advocates who argued that this interpretation was against the spirit of the ADA to provide equal access, and that not applying it to (new) online stores would shut people with disabilities out of a substantial portion of the economy.

Meeting regulatory requirements is a good first step but it is not a replacement for common sense, or enough to meet the real goal of making products delightful and usable for all. In Chapter 4, we'll cover how individual products can adapt guidelines and frameworks to meet the needs of their users.

But as a first step, it is essential to understand the difference between law, policy, and guidelines applicable to your business. For companies operating in different global markets, requirements might vary, and the best course of action is to check with the respective legal and regulatory teams.

---

[18]www.accenture.com/_acnmedia/pdf-89/accenture-disability-inclusion-research-report.pdf
[19]www.cnbc.com/2019/10/07/dominos-supreme-court.html

In the United States, there are four significant accessibility regulations: The 21st Century Video and Accessibility Act (CVAA), Section 508, and the Americans with Disabilities Act (ADA) applies to software product development.

I.   Web Content Accessibility Guidelines (WCAG)

The World Wide Web Consortium (W3C) is an international community where professional groups, companies, academic experts and industry experts, full-time staff, and the public work together to develop open Web Standards. The Web Accessibility Initiative within W3C develops standards and support materials to help understand and implement accessibility.

While WCAG guidelines are not regulatory requirements, they are commonly referenced by regulatory guidelines as a way to evaluate accessibility. They became the basis for Section 508 in the United States in 2017 and EN 301 549 used in Europe.[20] Additionally, the United Kingdom, Australia, and Canada reference WCAG as the standard for government-related websites. For example, government sites in the United Kingdom must strive for WCAG-level AA compliance.[21]

The WCAG guidelines are based on four principles, abbreviated as POUR:

- Perceivable

- Operable

- Understandable

- Robust

Software developers can meet the WCAG guidelines on three conformance levels in increasing order of accessibility:

- Level A (minimum)

- Level AA (more accessible), includes all level A guidelines

- Level AAA (enhanced), includes all AA guidelines

---

[20] www.w3.org/WAI/news/2018-09-13/WCAG-21-EN301549/

[21] www.gov.uk/guidance/accessibility-requirements-for-public-sector-websites-and-apps

We will unpack these guidelines in more detail in a later chapter and talk about when it makes sense to deviate from them. Another point to note is that these guidelines are evolving toward a different set of standards with WCAG 3.0.[22] These standards are meant to keep pace with changing technologies, encapsulate a wider set of user needs, and encourage products toward better accessibility, instead of meeting minimum requirements set by the previous version (WCAG 2.1).

II.   Section 508

Under this section of the U.S. Rehabilitation Act of 1973, as amended in 1998, all federally funded websites must conform to WCAG 2.0 Level AA success criteria. This includes government agencies and government-funded nonprofit organizations, public schools, and universities. It does not apply to private companies unless they receive federal funding or contracts.

III.   Americans with Disabilities Act

Since 1990, this civil rights law prohibits discrimination against individuals with disabilities in all areas of public life, including jobs, schools, transportation, and all public and private places that are open to the general public.

The ADA encompasses all private and public entities that are considered public accommodations. These include hotels, restaurants, grocery stores, banks, healthcare facilities, public transportation, schools, social services, and gyms.[23] This list includes digital public accommodations, not just physical ones (at least in many US jurisdictions).

IV.   The 21st Century Communications and Video Accessibility Act (CVAA)

The CVAA makes sure that accessibility laws enacted in the 1980s and 1990s are brought up to date with 21st century technologies, including new digital, broadband, and mobile innovations.[24]

---

[22] www.w3.org/TR/wcag-3.0/

[23] www.ada.gov/taman3.html

[24] www.fcc.gov/consumers/guides/21st-century-communications-and-video-accessibility-act-cvaa

This includes expanding closed captioning requirements for broadcast TV content to its Internet distribution, and for browsers and advanced communication services[25] (ACS) to be accessible by people with disabilities.

Let us now look at a few examples of regulations outside the United States:

I.   The European Web Accessibility Directive

This EU directive requires accessibility for all public sector websites. Other significant requirements include providing:

1.   A public accessibility statement

     An accessibility statement is a way for organizations to provide information about their content's accessibility, to show a commitment to accessibility, and to provide users with contact information in case they encounter problems.[26]

2.   A feedback mechanism for users to report inaccessible content.

3.   Regular monitoring of public sector websites and apps by member states and reporting on the results.[27]

II.   The European Accessibility Act

The European accessibility act passed in 2019[28] covers products and services that have been identified as being most important for persons with disabilities while being most likely to have diverging accessibility requirements across EU countries.

These products and services include computers and operating systems, smartphones, TV equipment related to digital television services, banking services, ebooks, and ecommerce, among others.

Transposition of the law to member countries must be completed by June 28, 2025, so the act is in effect, even though not enforceable until then. The main point is that it requires accessibility by private companies, while the Web Accessibility Directive is focused on public sector websites.

---

[25] www.fcc.gov/general/advanced-communications-services-acs
[26] www.w3.org/WAI/planning/statements/
[27] https://web-directive.eu/#toc1
[28] https://ec.europa.eu/social/main.jsp?catId=1202

III.   The Accessible Canada Act (ACA)

The ACA requires government websites to conform with WCAG 2.0 Level AA guidelines. Individual provinces are also enacting accessibility laws, some of which are under development. For example, Accessibility for Ontarians with Disabilities (AODA) aims to create a barrier-free Ontario by 2025. The AODA covers both public and private sector companies and can entail fines of $10,000 for each day of violation.[29]

IV.   GDPR, HIPAA, and Privacy Regulations

Data collection and privacy limitations vary by the markets, that is, geographies you serve. While these are not directly accessibility regulations, they influence the measurement and tracking of accessibility initiatives in consumer technology products.

Some regions might require special permission from the user. Others might restrict the collection of data or analysis of user behavior on products based on types of disabilities. One example of this in the United States is HIPAA[30] that prohibits collection and use of certain health-related data, which can be interpreted to mean disability data.

The General Data Protection Regulation (GDPR) is a law on data protection and privacy in the European Union (EU) that limits the collection of specific categories of personal data and gives users the right to control and manage their data. In certain countries, data related to disability is categorized as health data and is either not allowed for collection for general software providers or is highly restrictive in its provisions.[31]

Case Study: Data Visualization for the Blind

Let's walk-through a case study of a solution I designed and implemented with the Yahoo Finance and accessibility team in 2017 to demonstrate how going beyond basic compliance guidelines can move the status quo forward.

Figure 1-5 shows a line chart representing the stock price of Apple Inc. over a year. There are 365 data points, one for each day of the year, on a small section of the screen that give most users a summary of the trend. A sighted user can take one quick look at the chart and know that there was a significant dip in March and a significant rise in September of 2020.

---

[29] https://siteimprove.com/en-ca/blog/a-complete-overview-of-canada-s-accessibility-laws/

[30] www.hhs.gov/hipaa/for-professionals/privacy/laws-regulations/index.html

[31] https://gdpr-info.eu/

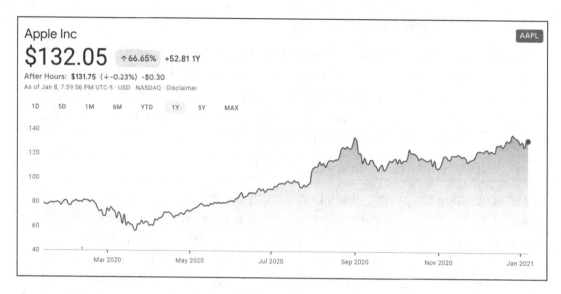

Figure 1-5. *A one-year Apple Stock chart from Google Finance Web[32] as of January 2021*

Now let's think about the experience for a user who is blind or visually impaired and relies on a screen reader.

Note   Screen readers are software programs that allow blind or visually impaired users to hear a description of what is displayed on the computer screen through a speech synthesizer or braille display. The user sends commands through touch-screen gestures or by pressing different combinations of keys on the computer keyboard or braille display to instruct the screen reader to speak.[33] Screen readers can be stand-alone programs, or built into the operating system. The three most common screen readers by usage are JAWS, NVDA, and VoiceOver.[34]

---

[32] www.google.com/finance/quote/AAPL:NASDAQ

[33] www.afb.org/blindness-and-low-vision/using-technology/assistive-technology-products/screen-readers

[34] https://webaim.org/projects/screenreadersurvey9/

Currently, the status quo for popular financial products is to either have the screen reader just skip over the chart or only read the chart title without any key data points. In the first instance, the screen reader user doesn't know there is a chart. In the second instance, they know there is a chart but not what it is trying to communicate. Obviously, both of these are highly undesirable experiences and vastly different from the experience of sighted people. This is likely because of the reasons discussed in Chapter 1 – prioritization and technical difficulty of implementing a better solution.

The recommended best practice for screen reader access to data visualizations is to speak a description of the directional trend,[35] and as a next step, speak the data as if it were a table. This is the equivalent of showing a sighted user something like Table 1-1 instead of a chart:

Table 1-1. *Table with two columns – date and the corresponding stock price from 2020 to 2021 in each row*

Date	Price
2020-01-13	79.239998
2020-01-14	78.169998
2020-01-15	77.834999
2020-01-16	78.809998
2020-01-17	79.682503
2020-01-21	79.142502
2020-01-22	79.425003
2020-01-23	79.807503
2020-01-24	79.577499
2020-01-27	77.237503
2021-01-06	126.599998
2021-01-07	130.919998
2021-01-08	132.050003

---

[35] https://accessibility.psu.edu/images/charts/

While this is an improvement from just speaking a description, it is not even close to the experience of getting a quick summary from large amounts of data a sighted user could glean in a few seconds. A few applications such as Google Finance extract key data points, including the high, low, and the previous close price, which is a great improvement over the table-like structure. However, it still doesn't give the user the option to interact with all data points and interact with data points that *they* may find interesting besides those chosen for them.

Can we do better? Of course, we can. As one of my mentors, Jean-Baptiste Quéru pointed out, "Being the best at something doesn't mean you're good at it." This is a case where going beyond, or deviating from the guidelines leads to a better experience.

The thought process for most accessibility solutions includes leveraging the physical cognitive and sensory capabilities that are available to the user. In the case of blindness, we use sounds and haptics (touch) to convey information that cannot be accessed visually.

Figure 1-6 shows how the experience looks visually. To watch the feature in action, visit `www.youtube.com/watch?v=d_c-auuDsz`

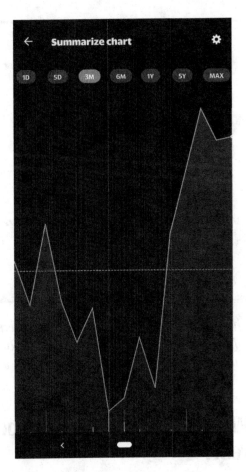

Figure 1-6. *Audio chart screenshot from the Yahoo Finance Android app over a three-month period trending upward, with five dips in the middle and a horizontal line representing the previous close price*

Let us now break down the experience and why these design and implementation choices were made.

Step 1: How Do We Summarize the Information Without a Visual Representation?

Using music, more specifically tones that vary in pitch as the price goes up and down, can help users who are able to recognize these differences get a quick summary of the trend of the data. In user studies my team conducted with users with blindness, about 80% of people tested could draw the overall pattern after listening to the corresponding tones. Figure 1-7 shows an image with a sample of those drawings from real users.

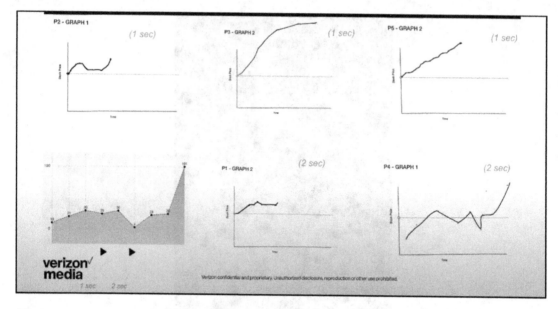

Figure 1-7. *Reference chart with drawings by five users during a research session held to test the efficacy of the audio-haptic charts solution for users with low vision. All drew an upward trending chart*

Step 2: How Do We Let the User Dive Deeper into the Data at Points of Interest?

Just like scrubbing through a video or audio file to skip to a specific time, we play the tones and read aloud the data points when a user decides to stop exploring the chart with their screen reader. Once the user is in this mode, navigating forward and backward reads the data like a table – a pattern they are already familiar with. When they are ready to explore the overall trend, they can start scrubbing again to hear the tones.

Step 3: Why Do We Need a Chart on the Screen If the User Is Blind?

The experience is not designed just for users with complete blindness. Low vision, partially sighted, or users with other visual impairments might be able to see the screen to some extent, and for them to hear a table while looking at a chart can be cognitively dissonant. If a sighted person is assisting a blind or visually impaired user with the application, they will benefit from the visual presentation too.

18

Step 4: Why a Dedicated, Full-Screen Experience?

When I conducted a user study on this feature, one finding was that blind users could not maintain contact with the same spatial position on the screen. For example, if they were exploring something in the first third of the screen, once they lifted their finger, it was difficult to tap that area with accuracy again.

This is why the chart experience, which is already data-dense and supports multiple interactions, was made full-screen. Users would know that the range is edge-to-edge, providing useful orientation, and leaving less room for accidentally activating an unintended onscreen element.

The implementation is made possible by overlaying invisible elements over the chart that correspond to the data points that are highlighted when the user stops. The project is made for Android and is open source. You can check it out here `https://github.com/yahoo/SongbirdCharts`. Since iOS 15 Apple provides an API for supporting audio charts with VoiceOver.[36] The API returns key semantic information to the user such as the minimum, maximum, and average. Developers on both iOS and Android products (99.4% of the mobile market) have freely available tools to support a better charts experience for blind users.

Step 5: What Are the Options for Customization?

In the default version, we chose the usually pleasant range of human audible frequency between 200 and 750 Hz. However, users reported that they wanted control over the range of pitch available to them based on their preference and hearing abilities.

Another option for customization derived from the format in which the data is read. The user can choose if they prefer the x-axis, that is, the time, to be read or not, and if so, the level of detail. This is important because if they are exploring data points one by one, long descriptions that are repetitive can be disruptive to the experience.

We also switched the order of the buttons that enable switching between ranges, so the user did not have to go through the chart before picking the range.

---

[36] `https://developer.apple.com/documentation/accessibility/axchart`

Step 6: How Else Can We Make This Better?

Before the user dives into the experience, it is often helpful to give them a summary of the data they might be looking for. In the case of financial charts, four data points that most users are interested in are the previous day's price, the highest price, the lowest price, and the current price over the range they have selected.

We read this information as soon as the user focuses their screen reader on the chart, along with the name of the stock and the currently selected time range. In addition, if the user decides to navigate by heading instead of using the default setting, they can skip through these data points on the chart without having to parse through the entire dataset.

The use of haptics or vibration provides reinforcement. It conveys to the user points of importance or gives them feedback when they stop after scrubbing and listening to tones.

Another layer of information in the case of financial charts comes from whether the current data point is above or below the previous closing price, something that traders care about. It is drawn as a horizontal line as shown in Figure 1-8.

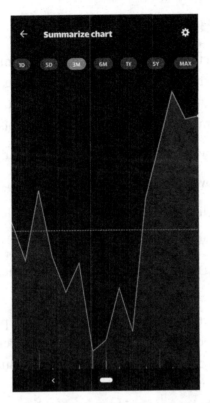

Figure 1-8. *Audio chart screenshot from the Yahoo Finance Android app over a three-month period trending upward, with five dips in the middle and a horizontal line representing the previous close price*

In this experience, we use the texture of sound to add an echo when the user is interacting with data points below the closing price vs. above. The echo can be turned off if the user finds it distracting – always an important option when introducing innovative new features or enhancements.

Case Study Takeaway

Although this example focused on stock charts, the principles are also applicable to charts beyond the financial markets world. In fact, a larger application could be in Education where blind students cannot interpret visual information as easily as their sighted counterparts. Each application will have nuances and optimizations that are specific to the context and user. That is the essence of accessibility. However, the more you think past simply following guidelines to achieve a general level of accessibility, the greater the reward in terms of an experience that can be genuinely enjoyable for everyone.

The Greatest Challenge

Suppose you ask any product team whether they care about making their product accessible or if it is an important area to focus on. In that case, you will almost always get a similar response to "Absolutely, but we don't know where to begin." Depending on who you speak to, this response might mean one or more of the following:

- We don't know how people with disabilities use our product

- We don't know how to assign priority to accessibility initiatives

- We read the guidelines but don't know how to implement solutions

- We don't know how to test or validate solutions

- We are developing mobile or other non-web products, what should we do?

At most academic institutions training future technology professionals, learning about accessibility is not a requirement, so knowledge is scarce. People with disabilities are also often not represented in the technology workforce. Building inclusively, therefore, requires unlearning years of practice without these considerations. The good news is that none of these challenges are insurmountable.

While having every possible user need represented within a team or even a company is impossible, we can engage people with lived experience in our processes. One of the greatest gifts we have as humans is the ability to empathize with others who might not share the same background, needs, and challenges as us. Putting yourself in temporary situations where you might experience a disability is at least one step closer to lived experience than no experience at all. Insights from these experiences are extremely powerful when combined with observations from real users, in realizing the full potential of our products.

In the following chapters, we will go over concepts, principles, and actionable steps to address each of these questions. Chapter 2 will answer the critical question that helps drive investment in accessibility – how do we measure impact and prioritize? Chapter 3 will cover the overall product development lifecycle, and the various business functions involved.

In Chapter 4, we will deep dive into the specifics of implementation on platforms that are not as well documented as the web, with examples. Chapters 5 and 6 will go in-depth on testing for accessibility, including automated and manual testing to close the loop on building maintainable, accessible products.

Lastly, we will discuss cutting-edge developments in the accessibility space and how emerging technologies such as augmented reality (AR), extended reality (XR), mixed reality (MR), and virtual reality (VR) will change the future of assistive technology.

Solving for accessibility at scale is still a relatively new field and something companies may be conscious of, but perhaps not actively addressing. Challenges around education, documentation, automation, handling of accessibility data, and personalization to meet users' unique needs make the space ripe for disruption. This is why, as we discuss best practices, we will also uncover opportunities for innovation.

Mobile Focus

The examples and case studies in this book will focus on mobile experiences instead of web or desktop for the following reasons:

1. Financial accessibility and mobile as a growth opportunity

The World Advertising Research Center predicts that 72% of all Internet users will use only their smartphones to access the web by 2025.[37] Mobile phones[38] are the most financially accessible means to interact with the online world, *and* the most convenient. Android phones are available for as low as $20.[39]

Mobile devices come equipped with sensors that leverage location, biomarkers (facial recognition, heart rate, etc.), visual, and sound cues to enable experiences that haven't traditionally been possible. For instance, six out of ten smartphone users have tried voice search in the past year.[40] Furthermore, mobile has unlocked whole new industries. For example, apps such as Uber and Lyft (highly successful ride-hailing apps used worldwide) wouldn't exist without mobile. Wearables and mobile payments add even newer dimensions to how enveloped mobile experiences are in our daily lives. The size of the mobile payments market is projected to increase at a 30% annual rate to reach $12 trillion by 2027[41] (Figure 1-9).

---

[37] www.cnbc.com/2019/01/24/smartphones-72percent-of-people-will-use-only-mobile-for-internet-by-2025.html

[38] In terms of operating systems, we will only cover iOS (Apple) and Android devices since they make up 99.3% of the smartphone market#, with Android at about 70%. www.statista.com/statistics/272698/global-market-share-held-by-mobile-operating-systems-since-2009/

[39] www.techradar.com/news/the-land-of-the-20-smartphone

[40] www.oberlo.com/blog/mobile-usage-statistics

[41] www.alliedmarketresearch.com/mobile-payments-market

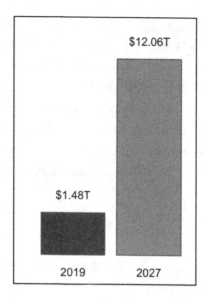

Figure 1-9. *The projected size of the mobile payments market to $12.06 trillion by 2027*

2. Mobile-specific challenges

While the intent and principles of website accessibility apply to all devices, there are specific challenges for mobile, including typically smaller screen sizes, touchscreen interfaces, network connectivity, and what *mobile* even encompasses – phones, wearables, and car devices, among others. In most cases, if an application is built to be accessible on mobile, it will be accessible on larger devices as well. We will discuss in detail a few examples of what makes mobile accessibility especially tricky in Chapter 3.

3. Accessibility Documentation of mobile development and design paradigms are years behind actual practice

Given that mobile is a relatively new space compared to the web, building mobile applications inclusively is far less well documented in the existing literature. The first and latest WCAG guidelines for mobile were released in 2015,[42] 16 years after the web version in 1999, and 8 years after the first iPhone was released. While the guidelines still hold, the mobile space has evolved with completely new interaction patterns, tooling, and design paradigms. A new set of guidelines for mobile is underway alongside WCAG

---

[42] www.w3.org/TR/mobile-accessibility-mapping/

4. Mobile encompasses web and native applications. Native applications are applications developed specifically for the platform. Unlike the web, which is device and operating system agnostic, native applications developed for Android cannot be installed on iPhones and vice versa.

The definition of mobile covers phones, tablets, and wearables. If a website is optimized to be accessible on these, it will only perform better on a larger surface with more computing power. This includes both the UI (user interface) and factors that make mobile devices financially accessible, such as network usage, battery consumption, and memory utilization.

Summary

- Over 97% of the world's top 1,000,000 websites fail basic automated audits to ensure it is usable by those with visual, auditory, physical, speech, cognitive, language, learning, and neurological disabilities.

- The goal of accessibility compliance is to ensure that providers meet the *minimum* set of requirements. That is not the same as being truly usable.

- As seen in the Yahoo Finance app case study, simply the following compliance would've meant enabling a screen reader, even though this would not allow a blind user to access the information quickly or with ease. The mobile app team chose to implement a feature allowing users to scrub through audio tones representing the data.

- In the United States, the three most significant accessibility standards are CVAA, Section 508, and the Americans with Disabilities Act (ADA). While WCAG are not legal requirements in the United States, they serve as the basis for Section 508 of the Rehabilitation Act update of 1998.

- This book will focus on mobile, because mobile phones and wearables are the fastest growing and most financially accessible means to interact with the online world, because of the specific challenges of mobile app accessibility, and because it has less well-documented guidelines.

CHAPTER 2

The Chicken or the Egg?

In the last chapter, we discussed the scale and potential impact of making technology products accessible for everyone. We saw that there is a mismatch between the desire to make accessible products, and the outcome, which is that 97% of the world's top 1,000,000 websites are still inaccessible.

One of the key reasons we identified was that it is difficult to prioritize accessibility initiatives without clear measures of progress, and it is difficult to see progress without prioritizing this work. In this chapter, we will look at qualitative and quantitative methods to measure impact.

Measuring Impact

One of the biggest challenges while building accessible products is prioritization. No decision-maker would say that they wouldn't like their application to be accessible. Doing so is the right thing to do, and most people want to do the right thing. It is a question of which right thing to do first, or ever, and the cost of doing so. Businesses are always performing ROI (return on investment) analysis.

Digital consumer products often measure results with metrics such as monthly (MAU) and daily active users (DAU) to indicate reach. Another widely used metric is the level of engagement of these users. This is often measured by metrics such as time spent, the number of clicks, and the number of sessions.

In the current technology landscape, most product managers and business stakeholders take pride in being data-driven. While data is a great decision-making tool, it can also be a crutch. Being able to accurately quantify the impact of individual features is powerful, but it should not come at the expense of sound product instincts and common sense. A long-term inclusive strategy and principled approach, with a short-term data compass, is what will take products beyond the status quo.

© Sukriti Chadha 2023
S. Chadha, *Beyond Accessibility Compliance*, https://doi.org/10.1007/978-1-4842-7948-9_2

As we mentioned in Chapter 1,

Impact = (People reached X Impact on each person) - (People excluded X Impact on each person)

Even though users with access needs might make a smaller percentage of a product's total audience, the impact on an untapped market that is not typically catered to is the balancing factor often not accounted for.

Both the number of users and their level of engagement are difficult to measure for people with disabilities because of the following:

1. *Privacy and data collection limitations*

It might be impossible to attribute the growth to accessibility efforts because, in some geographies, privacy laws prohibit the collection or analysis of disability data. For example, in the United Kingdom, disability data falls in a special category[1] and must meet special consent and processing requirements for its collection to be considered lawful.[2]

2. *Catch-22. How do we measure engagement for people we did not build for?*

To meaningfully engage with an application, a user must first be able to access it. It is difficult to measure the level of engagement among people with disabilities without first investing in building an accessible product.

3. *When data misleads*

Even after we overcome the above challenges, it is important to note that data is only useful if interpreted correctly. An example of this is the time spent by a user on the application in a single session. It is often a key metric that companies track to use as a proxy for engagement. In the case of people with disabilities, spending excessive time on parts of the application that should be relatively frictionless can be a false indicator of engagement, instead of a red flag indicating an inaccessible or poor user experience.

---

[1] https://ico.org.uk/for-organisations/guide-to-data-protection/guide-to-the-general-data-protection-regulation-gdpr/lawful-basis-for-processing/special-category-data/

[2] https://ico.org.uk/for-organisations/guide-to-data-protection/guide-to-the-general-data-protection-regulation-gdpr/lawful-basis-for-processing/special-category-data/

There's a good chance that you've experienced blockers like these before, or found yourself being asked (or asking) these sorts of questions. Now, let's revisit each of these obstacles in a way that allows us to overcome them.

- Qualitative analysis

The above example teaches us that data can be misleading if we look at raw numbers without connecting them to the user experience. For that reason, qualitative user studies are helpful in uncovering opportunities and bottlenecks in user flows that simply can't be inferred from quantitative methods alone. Learning from users with lived experience is the best way to understand how your product works for them.

In this section, we will focus on the usability research portion of UX (user experience) research. Two main methods to test for usability are lab studies (where users go through in-depth interviews on a few topics), and remote unmoderated studies (where users are asked to complete a task with their own devices in their natural environment, while their actions are recorded).

I witnessed the benefits of in-house state-of-the-art accessibility labs, fitted with a wide range of assistive technology equipment during my time at Yahoo. The primary use of the labs was for user researchers to conduct usability studies with people with disabilities. The head of accessibility led a brilliant initiative to make sure everyone hired at the company, regardless of their role, went through the lab in their first week. All employees knew that accessibility is a core part of the company culture and that they have a dedicated space to explore and empathize with assistive technology users. Developers, product managers, and designers often used the space.

Smaller companies might not have the expertise or resources to set up a dedicated lab and hire researchers who understand the nuances of studies with assistive technology. To solve this, there are companies such as Fable[3] that specialize in user interviews for people with disabilities, including remote interviews. In some countries such as the UK[4] and Australia,[5] government-run empathy labs are available for public use. There are also a few commercially available services that create temporary labs at office locations.

---

[3] https://makeitfable.com/

[4] https://gds.blog.gov.uk/2018/06/20/creating-the-uk-governments-accessibility-empathy-lab/

[5] www.nsw.gov.au/onecx/blog/empathy-lab-an-experience-enhances-accessibility-and-inclusive-design

If your company or team is unable to invest in any of the above ways, the next best type of qualitative research you can do is to put yourself in your users' shoes. Examples of this are changing the settings on your own device temporarily in the accessibility settings menu:

- Enlarging text

- Inverting colors

- Assistive touch

- Keyboard navigation (navigating a site without using a mouse)

- Screen reader (VoiceOver on Apple devices, and Talkback on Android devices)

Fun fact: Many of the settings that would reside in the accessibility menu are now part of general display settings (e.g., font size, magnification, color inversion), substantiating the argument that accessibility features benefit everyone.

- Between quantitative and qualitative measures: Extrapolation and proxy metrics

In cases where it is not possible to measure the reach of features built for people using assistive technology, it is still possible to make educated quantitative guesses.

To create tangible insights, you can use the data you already have about your audience, alongside trends reported by organizations such as the WHO (for global data), the CDC, and the American Foundation for the Blind (for the United States).

For instance, let's say you're trying to prioritize the importance of making a certain user flow[6] screen reader accessible (a tool used predominantly by those with visual impairments) on your mobile application in the United States.

Step 1: This report by the CDC[7] breaks down eye disorders by type and age group. From this, you get the age distribution of users with visual impairments who rely on screen readers to use your product.

---

[6] User flow is the path taken by a prototypical user on a website or app to complete a task. The user flow takes them from their entry point through a set of steps toward a successful outcome and final action, such as purchasing a product. (www.optimizely.com/optimization-glossary/)

[7] www.cdc.gov/visionhealth/risk/burden.htm

Step 2: This Statista report[8] then answers the question of how many users within these age groups use smartphones. Combining this with the information from the previous step gives you a rough estimate of potential reach.

Step 3: For your specific product space, there will either be industry reports or data you have gathered from your audience, that outline the characteristics of users interested in the product offering and their level of engagement. This will inform how representative of the overall market of consumers your user base is.

Step 4: You can now cross-reference these two datasets in order to estimate the potential impact on both the number of new users by investing in screen reader support, as well as engagement of existing users.

In this example, we looked at age. However, the same breakdown is possible on other parameters such as gender, geography, platform (web browser, operating system, etc.) interests, or other consumer cohorts.

- Quantitative analysis

Once you *are* able to collect data that helps you build aggregate cohorts of users with different types of disabilities, you can then go through the following steps:

1. Record the type of assistive technology a user has enabled on their device when they first launch a session of your application. These are called accessibility settings or services on different platforms, and they usually have APIs available to fetch these settings at an operating system level. An API (Application Programming Interface) is basically how two pieces of software share data.

One caveat of this method is that there isn't always a one-to-one mapping of the accessibility setting and the associated disability. For example, the Accessibility Service documentation for Android developers makes it possible to extract whether a specific setting such as magnification or color inversion is enabled.[9] These are buried in a list with less useful markers such as taps and swipes,[10] which don't indicate assistive technology use at all. The iOS documentation[11] is more digestible but has the same

---

[8] www.statista.com/statistics/489255/percentage-of-us-smartphone-owners-by-age-group/

[9] https://developer.android.com/reference/android/accessibilityservice/AccessibilityService

[10] Example, GESTURE_4_FINGER_SWIPE_RIGHT, which indicates a user has performed a 4 finger swipe

[11] https://developer.apple.com/documentation/uikit/uiaccessibility

limitation – you don't always know whether a user has a particular disability, multiple disabilities, or just a preference.

For example, magnification settings could be used by people with a variety of conditions including low vision, lack of fine motor skills, or cognitive challenges.

2. Instrument, or in other words, record interaction data such as clicks, scrolls, pinch to zoom, etc., on key user flows(if not *all* user flows) to understand conversion rates, engagement, and most importantly, task efficiency, that is, the time it takes a user to complete a given task. These interactions are typically tracked for all users in mature products. Task efficiency is a metric that can help break down dwell time into engagement and lag.

It's worth noting here that data related to assistive technology is restricted in many geographies, and for good reason – it can be considered sensitive, personal data and should be handled very carefully. While extracting insights from user journeys using this data at scale can be a powerful tool in helping product teams serve audiences with disabilities, mishandling or unintentional sharing with third parties can land you in unpleasant situations from both, a user trust standpoint, and a legal standpoint. Therefore if you're making use of this kind of data to understand and serve your audience better, do make sure this data is handled, stored, and shared with appropriate security measures in place.

- Negative impact

The previous methods discuss how to measure the impact of building inclusive products through increased reach and engagement, which are top-line metrics. Another way to look at measuring impact is to observe how deprioritizing inclusion hurts a company's brand value and exposes them to legal risk. As we saw, laws such as the Americans with Disabilities Act require service providers to build products that are accessible, and there are often severe consequences for those that don't. We can also look at the overhead of audits, retroactive bug-fixing, and reporting.

For benchmarking, Federal law allows fines of up to $75,000 for the first violation and $150,000 for additional ADA violations. States and local governments may allow additional fines and require businesses to meet a higher standard of accessibility than the ADA requires.[12]

---

[12] www.ada.gov/civil_penalties_2014.htm

One thing to note when avoiding bad PR or legal risk is the primary motivation for investment in accessibility is a bias toward short-term fixes to achieve compliance. This kind of myopic thinking is unfortunately very common, and routinely requires more work than tackling the underlying issues.

One might notice companies outsourcing audits and fixing "bugs" to reach compliance as quickly as possible. This leads to suboptimal band-aid solutions that may meet requirements but do not offer a great user experience. Worse still are accessibility overlays that promise to "work" out of the box, and offer immediate compliance. As we will cover in Chapter 4, doing accessibility right requires a 360-degree solution in the entire product life cycle. Bolt-on solutions are automated tools that cannot even detect a majority of issues let alone solve them. Additionally, they don't work on mobile and might even make your product experience worse.[13]

The more serious problem with these shortcuts is that teams typically spend way more time assigning, discussing, and fixing issues than they would had accessibility been part of the entire lifecycle from the start. A few major side effects of this reactionary approach are

1. End-users experience issues for longer, resulting in less engagement.

2. Legal and PR risk increases with the lifespan of the error.

3. Learnings from the audit remain localized instead of feeding back into the system to solve commonly occurring issues more holistically.

4. Teams lose ownership and miss the opportunity to learn from bugs they create because accessibility is now someone else's responsibility, leading them to creating more bugs that require future remediation.

5. The overhead of audits, reporting, communication, and releasing (especially for mobile products) is significant especially in larger, distributed development teams. Please refer to the note at the end of this chapter for an example of estimating the overhead and tradeoff with considering accessibility from the start.

---

[13] www.nytimes.com/2022/07/13/technology/ai-web-accessibility.html

6. The opportunity cost of losing customers who find the product inaccessible. Once we are able to decrypt data on assistive technology usage and drop-offs in user journeys, we can more accurately estimate this number, but below is a way to calculate the ballpark opportunity cost:

X = Monthly active users in a region/total population in the region
Y = Number of people with a disability related to existing issues
V = Lifetime value per user

$$\textbf{Opportunity cost} = \textbf{Y} * \textbf{X} * \textbf{LTV}$$

Lifetime value per user will vary depending on the product. One metric that can help estimate the upper bound of the lifetime value of a largely untapped market is disposable income, that is, the ability to spend.

In the United States, the total after-tax disposable income for working-age people with disabilities is about $490 billion, which is similar to that of other significant market segments, such as African Americans ($501 billion) and Hispanics ($582 billion).[14]

In the UK, in 2017, the value of the "purple pound" – in other words, the spending power of people with disabilities – was estimated at around £249 billion (over 300 billion USD).[15] A 2021 report[16] estimated that people with disabilities have nearly half a trillion dollars in disposable income – the after-tax dollars for basic necessities such as housing, food, and clothing.

- Additional Benefits

Fostering an inclusive culture that is consistently apparent in a company's product portfolio also pays off in long-term brand affinity and recruiting.

In my personal experience while working at Yahoo Finance, when my team was hiring mobile engineers, we found candidates that explicitly called out our focus on accessibility as a reason for their interest in the role. To these candidates, it was a strong indicator of an inclusive environment. They knew a team that values diversity of experience and users of its products is also more likely to be open to their new ideas and diverse opinions.

---

[14] www.air.org/resource/report/hidden-market-purchasing-power-working-age-adults-disabilities

[15] www.bbc.com/news/av/business-39040760

[16] https://iel.org/purchasing-power-people-disabilities

The same goes for customers and other stakeholders. Many people have a friend or family member that lives with a disability given that one in four people have one. It is obvious that we will feel a higher brand affinity to products that go above and beyond to include our loved ones. One example is Mars' award-winning *Look on the Light Side* campaign,[17] that increased brand affinity by 20%.

What About Products Already on the Market?

While ideally, products are accessible when they are released, most products are already in the hands of users by the time product teams realize they missed accessibility considerations. Often, this comes after users file complaints, or report bugs on social media. At this point, companies typically either allocate resources for a set of experts to form a central accessibility team or outsource the function to third parties.

Depending on the size of the company and available resources, either choice can work. In the short term, because accessibility is an unfamiliar domain for most technology professionals, it is important to rely on subject matter experts who can identify, prioritize, and provide specific guidance. In the long term though, the goal should be for product development teams to save time and money by learning to do this work themselves, and to look at accessibility as an avenue for growth and product differentiation.

As a result, Chapter 4 will look at implementing this two-part strategy:

1) Addressing existing issues

2) Developing a sustainable accessibility strategy to

   (a). Avoid regressions

   (b). Build products inclusively from the start

First though, we will look at how functional needs vary for different sets of users.

---

[17] www.smartcitieslibrary.com/the-importance-of-being-a-disability-inclusive-brand-ogilvy-com/

Note on Roughly Quantifying Overhead of Audits

a. Audits can be as expensive as $20,000 to $50,000 for a single project (e.g., a single website, Android app, iOS app), and take weeks to conduct. Most good tech companies release several versions of their products in that timeframe. Waiting for audits means either slowing down your release cycle, or rendering the findings irrelevant, and the money wasted.

b. Let's say the audit reports 20 issues, each of which requires two hours (conservative estimate) of the following people's time to fix on average

   1. Product manager or subject matter expert to triage

   2. Project manager to assign to teams

   3. Designer to redesign

   4. Engineer to fix

   5. QA to verify

Taking $50/hr as a conservative estimate based on a publicly available web engineer's salary[18] as the basis for this time, 20 issues will cost the team

20 issues * 2 hours per issue * $50 per hour * 5 people = $10,000

This, plus the cost of the audit comes to about $20,000-$50,000. On three platforms (web, iOS, and Android), that adds up to an upper bound of $150,000. Even if we account for audits once a quarter, this adds up to about

$600,000/year

Alternatively, let us assume that adding inclusive practices as part of your overall workflow takes 20% more of these people's time (anecdotally, the number is about 5-10%). The rough estimate of that comes out to

0.2*100,000 (based on $50/hr)*5 = $100,000/year

---

[18] www.ziprecruiter.com/Salaries/Software-Engineer-Salary-per-Hour

Summary

- The number of users and their level of engagement are difficult to measure for people with disabilities with traditional metrics because of privacy and data collection limitations, unavailable data due to historical lack of prioritization, and nuanced interpretation of collected data.

- Qualitative user studies uncover opportunities and bottlenecks in user flows that can't be inferred from quantitative methods alone. Learning from users with lived experience is the best way to understand how your product works for them.

- Two key methods to test for usability are lab studies, where users go through in-depth interviews on a few topics, and remote unmoderated studies, where users are asked to complete a task with their own devices in their natural environment, while their actions are recorded.

- The next best type of qualitative research you can do is to put yourself in your users' shoes by temporarily enabling accessibility settings such as a screen reader, inverted colors, or enlarged text.

- To make educated quantitative guesses, you can use the data you already have about your audience, alongside trends reported by organizations such as the CDC and the American Foundation for the Blind.

- The problem with shortcuts such as outsourced audits is that teams spend way more time assigning, discussing, and fixing issues than they would had accessibility been part of the entire lifecycle from the start.

- Fostering an inclusive culture that is apparent in a company's product can also pay off in long-term brand affinity and recruiting.

CHAPTER 3

The Basics: Functional User Needs and Common Solutions

In Chapter 1, we briefly talked about how the greatest challenge after prioritization is that teams often do not have experience with accessibility and assistive technologies.

In this chapter, we will walk-through concrete examples of user needs that apply to mobile and web interfaces for different subsets of disabilities. In each case, we will also uncover growth opportunities made possible by accounting for these needs.

User Needs by Type of Disability and Examples of Assistive Technologies

In this section, we will walk-through concrete examples of user needs that map roughly to Web Content Accessibility Guidelines (WCAG) level A and AA. We briefly covered the WCAG in Chapter 1. WCAG is an ever-evolving comprehensive set of guidelines best referenced at w3c.org. We will not cover each guideline of the WCAG here. Instead, we will discuss different types of disabilities and how to think about basic user needs for each. Once you have a foundational understanding of user needs broken down by type of disability, you will be much better equipped to address more complex user needs, for example, for people with overlapping disabilities.

© Sukriti Chadha 2023
S. Chadha, *Beyond Accessibility Compliance*, https://doi.org/10.1007/978-1-4842-7948-9_3

People with Visual Impairments

Visual impairments encompass blindness, partial vision loss, color blindness, and light sensitivity, among other conditions. In the United States alone, 12 million people over the age of 40 have a visual impairment, including 1 million who are blind.[1] There are also millions of people who prefer to read larger or smaller text, use alternative color themes like Window High Contrast Mode or dark mode, or voice commands.

The most common type of assistive technology used by people with complete or partial blindness is screen readers. Screen readers output the contents on a digital device as speech or braille. The first screen reader was developed in 1986 at IBM.[2] Today, most devices come preloaded with a free screen reader. Some of the most popular screen readers are NVDA,[3] JAWS,[4] VoiceOver (Apple products), and TalkBack (Android).

About 8% of males and 0.5% of females suffer from a condition called "red-green" color vision deficiency,[5] which makes the perception of red or green difficult. For people with color blindness or light sensitivity, settings such as dark mode, brightness, or color inversion are other forms of assistive technology.

Below are a few basic guidelines that apply primarily to making products accessible for people with visual impairments:

Alternative Text

All non-text content, images, and actionable components are labeled with descriptive alternative text unless they are purely decorative. Screen readers use the alternative text provided by the website or application to read to the user when the user focuses on a component. Following is how this looks on a website (Figure 3-1), on Android (Figure 3-2), and on iOS (Figure 3-3), along with code samples for each:

---

[1] cdc.gov/visionhealth/basics/ced/fastfacts.htm

[2] https://knowbility.org/blog/2021/a-brief-history-of-screen-readers

[3] www.nvaccess.org/about-nvda/

[4] www.freedomscientific.com/products/software/jaws/

[5] www.nhs.uk/conditions/colour-vision-deficiency/

Figure 3-1. *Web page with an image in current focus*

Web:

```
<img src="bedroom.png" alt="A bedroom in a remote cabin with a bed, table,
and two windows">
```

Figure 3-2. *Android app screen with an image card in current focus*

Android:

```
<ImageView
  ...
  android:id="@+id/detail1" />
  android:contentDescription=""A bedroom in a remote cabin with a bed,
  table, and two windows" />
```

Or

```
<ImageView
  ...
  android:id="@+id/detail1" />
  android:contentDescription="A bedroom in a remote cabin with a bed, table,
  and two windows" />
```

Figure 3-3. *iOS app screen with an image card in current focus*

iOS:

```
extension RecipeCell {
  func applyAccessibility(_ recipe: Recipe) {

  foodImageView.accessibilityTraits = .image
  foodImageView.accessibilityLabel ="A bedroom in a remote cabin with a bed,
  table, and two windows"
```

Or

```
extension RecipeCell {
  func applyAccessibility(_ recipe: Recipe) {

  foodImageView.accessibilityTraits = .image
  foodImageView.accessibilityLabel = "A bedroom in a remote cabin with a
  bed, table, and two windows"
```

Note   In all the preceding three code samples, we used the English description. In applications that serve a global audience, we would replace the English text with a variable that assigns localized text according to a user's location and language preferences.

Adding a label is not enough to make the experience usable. It should describe what the component is, if it is in a particular state (if the element represents a state of the application), and what action a user can take (if applicable). For example, if a checkbox or toggle component is selected or unselected, the state should be read with the description. For a volume slider on an audio component, the percentage or value of where the user is should be read with the description.

What about user-generated content?

In the above example, all of the content is provided by the application creator. When the content is user generated, for example on social media platforms, we have two options:

1. Encouraging users to add alternative text at the upload stage or later

Twitter is a great example of this. As shown in Figure 3-4, as of 2020,[6] the platform has an "+Alt" button always visible when posting a tweet with an image that lets the uploader add a label.

---

[6] https://twitter.com/TwitterA11y/status/1265689579371323392?s=20

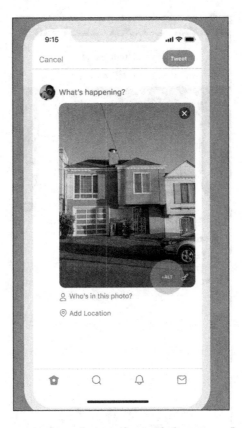

Figure 3-4. *Image of a tweet that shows the +Alt button when someone is uploading an image to Twitter*

2. Use image recognition to generate captions/alternate text for visual assets (Figure 3-5).

Figure 3-5. *Android app screen with an image card in current focus*

Image Processing and Machine Learning in Action

If the images are baked into the application, adding alternative text is pretty straightforward. If the content is user generated, for example on Facebook or Instagram, where users are posting their own content, the product can use image recognition to provide labels for images that don't have captions as a fallback to (or to enhance) captions supplied by the user uploading.

In 2016, Facebook (now Meta) released a feature for users with visual impairments that uses neural networks to recognize faces and objects in images. In 2017, the company launched a feature for everyone which automatically tags people in photos using facial recognition. This technology detects people, objects, scenes, actions, places of interest, and whether an image or video contains objectionable content.[7] With over 250 billion photos on the platform,[8] you can imagine the enormous amounts of data such a feature generates, as well as its endless applications in search, content moderation, and ads personalization while providing a richer, more powerful experience for users with visual impairments.

Meaningful Sequence, Grouping, and Hierarchy

Screen readers allow navigation by headings, links, paragraphs, and other structural attributes. In order for them to work as expected, these elements must be programmatically identifiable, and in a focus order that is consistent with the intent of the content.

In the following example (Figure 3-6), reading the image description of the sofa, followed by the title and price might be confusing and repetitive. Even though visually the title appears after the image, it should be the first thing read to the user. To make the experience even better, the title, image description, and price should be grouped together so the user does not have to focus on three items to get information that is part of one item.

---

[7] https://engineering.fb.com/2016/04/04/ios/under-the-hood-building-accessibility-tools-for-the-visually-impaired-on-facebook/

[8] https://www.brandwatch.com/blog/facebook-statistics/

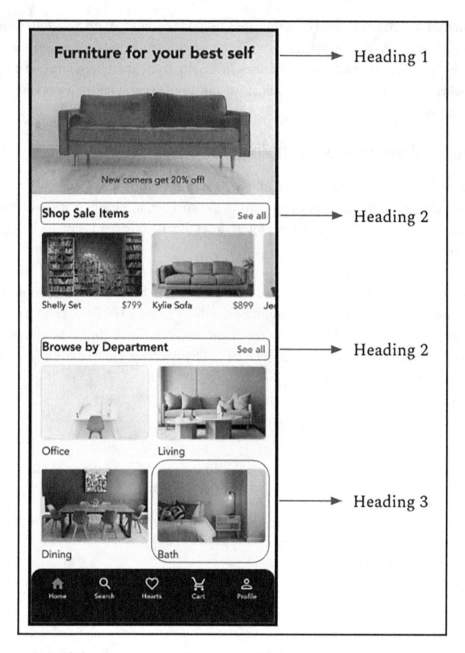

Figure 3-6. *Mobile app screen with images of furniture, with sale items and departments as subcategories*

In terms of hierarchy, the page title is first, followed by the section headings "Shop Sale Items" and "Browse by Department," followed by department cards such as "Office," "Living," "Dining," and "Bath," and finally the individual items under the sale tab.

Pages themselves are given descriptive titles too – this serves the same purpose as when a sighted user looks at the header of a page and decides whether they want to spend more time on it. For the same reason, another important detail to include with page titles, especially when a user first lands on an application is the language of the page. It is as easy as adding the following lines of code on web pages:

```
<html lang="en">
<head>
 <title>Page Title</title>
</head>
```

On iOS apps, add the following line to your View Controller's function:

```
override func viewDidLoad() {
 super.viewDidLoad()
 self.title = "Page Title"
}
```

On Android apps, add the following line to your activity's XML file or in code:

```
getActivity().setTitle("Page Title");
```

Not convinced? No worries. Search engines use text, headings,[9] titles, alternative text, and page structure to determine search ranking. If your site isn't taking meaningful hierarchy and headings into account, you won't be getting many visitors anyway.

Dynamic Sizing

Users can adjust the size of text and other components such as images. The WCAG guideline for text resizing allows up to a 200% increase in size without the use of assistive technology. This guideline also helps people with motor disabilities such as tremors, who might have trouble reliably tapping a small target area.

---

[9] https://www.searchenginejournal.com/on-page-seo/header-tags/

If the viewports are not restricted in both directions, that is, horizontally and vertically, such that overflowing content wraps in one direction, most dynamic sizing issues can be resolved. Restricting the flow of content to either vertical or horizontal scrolling (also known as reflow[10]) makes it easier for people with vision loss (who need enlarged text) and with motor impairments to track and easily read the content.

In Figures 3-7 and 3-8, we have two examples of potential issues that can arise in apps when the user increases their font size and magnification. The device will take all the text and enlarge it, but if the surrounding UI elements don't adapt to this change, we might end up with an indecipherable experience such as the one in Figure 3-7.

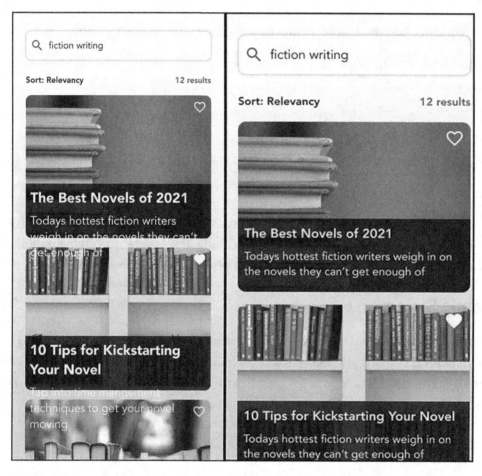

Figure 3-7. *Two mobile app screens. One on the left with a large text size, where images don't scale with the text, causes elements to overlap, making it unreadable. One on the right, where the rest of the content scales with enlarged text*

---

[10] https://www.w3.org/WAI/WCAG21/Understanding/reflow.html

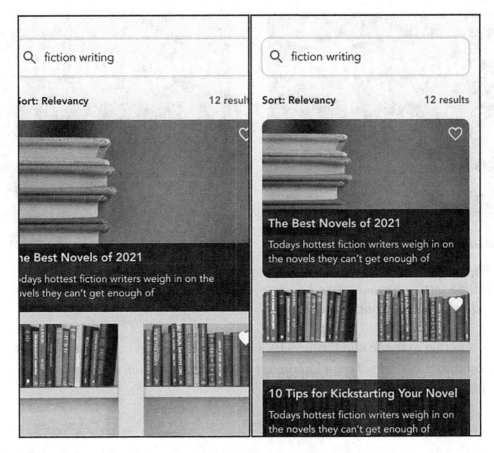

Figure 3-8. *Two mobile app screens. One on the left is a small device screen where horizontal content gets cut off instead of vertically scaling. One on the right depicts a large device and content showing as intended*

Colors Alone Are Not Used to Convey Meaning

Content and instructions if conveyed through color, shape, size, or other solely visual means should have text equivalents or another marker.

For example, on a Spotify playlist, a dot below the shuffle button, in addition to the changed color represents the current status of the setting as shown in Figure 3-9.

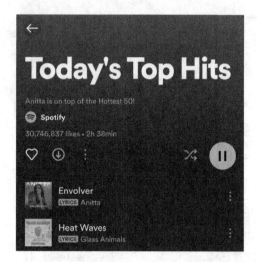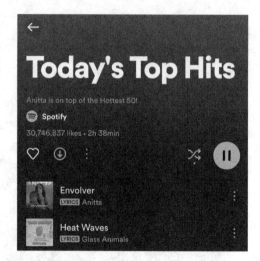

Figure 3-9. *A side-by-side comparison of a Spotify playlist page with the shuffle setting turned off and on respectively. The shuffle button turns green with a dot on the bottom when on*

Another example is in Figure 3-10, a user with red-green color blindness (the most common strain of color blindness) will not be able to tell which stocks have had a positive or negative movement.

Figure 3-10. *List of financial stocks where a positive movement is shown by a green background and negative movement by a red background*

However, in Figure 3-11, the simple addition of the plus and minus characters provides a way of understanding whether a stock has risen or fallen without relying on color to convey that meaning.

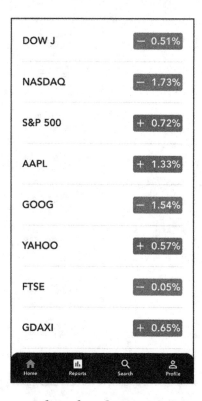

Figure 3-11.   *List of financial stocks where a positive movement is shown by a green background and a + symbol and negative movement by a red background and a - symbol*

Note that the same colors might have different meanings in different cultures. For example, the color red has a positive connotation in Chinese culture, and that is reflected in how stock price movements are presented on the Apple stocks app in China (Figure 3-12).

Figure 3-12. *List of financial stocks where a positive movement is shown by a red background and a + symbol and negative movement by a green background and a - symbol for users in China[11]*

Most mobile devices also have dark mode and settings such as color inversion in their accessibility menu, that transform all colors specified in the code of an app or website. We have the following two images: one where images and videos are excluded from color inversion (Figure 3-13), and one where they are not (Figure 3-14).

---

[11] https://twitter.com/Valzevul/status/1217412988149338117?s=20

Figure 3-13. *Mobile screen with inverted colors where the video is excluded from color inversion*

Figure 3-14. *Mobile screen with inverted colors where the video is not excluded from color inversion*

Links and Other Actions That Lead to Context Change Have Clear Descriptions

Links or components that redirect a user to a page other than the one they are currently on, or that change the context must have a clear purpose and a way to revert the action if accidentally activated, such as with a back button. Links should also be visually distinguishable from regular text, either with an underline or another marker so it is clear that they are actionable elements, and with text that describes what the link is, instead of the commonly used "Read More" or "Here" links. The reason for this is that screen reader users can navigate by links, and nondescript links read out of context are not helpful. Figure 3-15 shows an example of a link within a block of text.

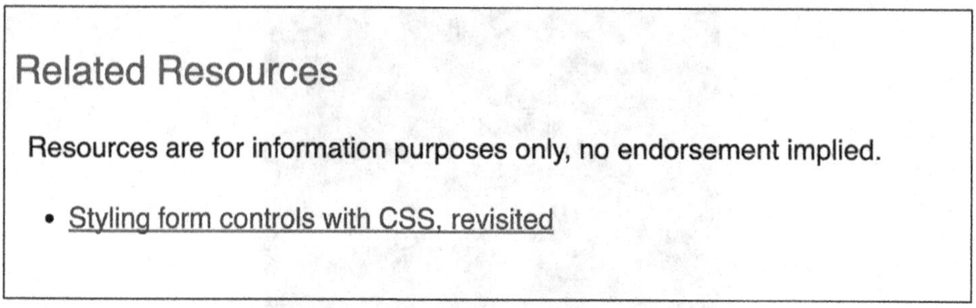

Related Resources

Resources are for information purposes only, no endorsement implied.

- Styling form controls with CSS, revisited

Figure 3-15. *Text box with a link to "Styling form controls with CSS, revisited" where the link text is underlined and marked with a different color (blue) than regular text[12]*

An Auto-playing Video or Audio Should Not Interfere with the Screen Reader

This guideline requires that you provide user controls for auto-playing files if the content is played for more than three seconds since the sound from the file can interfere with the screen reader.[13]

Synchronized Video Content Has Audio Descriptions

If there are movements or context changes in a movie scene while there is no sound, audio descriptions are the only way for blind users to follow along with their sighted counterparts.

Beyond Compliance

Aside from the benefits to people with permanent visual impairments, here are a few other use cases and opportunities unlocked by the above guidelines:

Defaulting to no volume regardless of video duration and letting the user decide whether a file should be played with the sound on is a better experience for everyone. Overall, auto-playing videos are quickly going out of style as people are realizing their

---

[12] https://www.w3.org/WAI/WCAG21/Understanding/focus-visible.html

[13] www.w3.org/TR/UNDERSTANDING-WCAG20/visual-audio-contrast-dis-audio.html

accessibility pitfalls, as well as their adverse business repercussions.[14] Auto-play also increases page load times, adds cognitive load, and introduces unnecessary data usage.

If an application supports voice interaction and audio descriptions, it is safer and more accessible while driving. The same goes for use of voice assistants such as home speakers without screens.

People might just prefer larger or smaller text sizes, regardless of disability. We have all at some point, zoomed into a block of text on our phones or changed the font size on our Kindle devices.[15] Some people prefer smaller text sizes so they can fit more content on a given screen, especially on mobile devices.

Accounting for dynamic views depending on magnification also allows for expansion to other languages that might require different screen space compared to the default.

Additionally, descriptions for images and audio descriptions for videos make content more discoverable given that search engines use alt text along with other metadata to rank and show images in search results.[16]

People with Hearing Impairment

Hearing impairment, similar to visual impairment, could mean complete loss of hearing, unilateral loss (in one ear), or partial deafness. In the United States alone, over 30[17] million people have hearing impairments, with over 11 million people who are deaf or have serious hearing limitations.[18] This excludes millions of people with partial hearing loss or less severe conditions who would benefit from having access to a different modality than sound.

Assistive technology used by people with hearing loss includes hearing aids, captions, and transcripts. Things to keep in mind for making products more accessible to this cohort of users are as follows.

---

[14] https://wistia.com/learn/marketing/against-autoplaying-homepage-videos

[15] E-reader device sold by Amazon

[16] https://developers.google.com/search/docs/advanced/guidelines/google-images

[17] www.nidcd.nih.gov/health/statistics/quick-statistics-hearing

[18] https://infoguides.rit.edu/c.php?g=380750&p=2706325

Audio and Video Content Include Captions

Note   *Audio descriptions (covered in the section on visual impairments), closed captions, and subtitles are sometimes used interchangeably, even though they are meant for different use cases. Audio descriptions include (in addition to the original soundtrack), a description of what is happening visually.[19] Closed captions assume that the user cannot hear, and include background sounds along with speaker changes and text. Subtitles assume that the user is hearing and only include spoken dialogue. A transcript is a text file with the spoken dialogue in the entire video or audio file, but not part of the video/audio file. It may or may not have speaker labels, time stamps, and audio descriptions.*

The Telecommunications Act of 1996 in the United States requires broadcasters, cable companies, and satellite television service providers to provide closed captioning for 100% of all new, nonexempt, English-language video programming.[20]

Captions or transcripts can be manually generated, for instance, by creating a WebVTT file[21] or with ASR (Automatic Speech Recognition). The trade-offs between manual and ASR options are price, speed (turnaround time), and most importantly accuracy. Depending on the quality of the audio file (background noise, number of speakers, recording equipment, etc.), the accuracy of ASR captions can drop significantly.[22] The accuracy of speech-to-text systems is typically measured by WER (Word Error Rate), that is, the percentage of transcription errors a system makes. A word error rate of 5-10% is considered good.[23] Acceptable error tolerance will of course depend on the application and the brand using ASR models.

---

[19] https://accessible360.com/accessible360-blog/2020-03-04-closed-captioning-vs-audio-descriptions/

[20] www.nad.org/resources/technology/television-and-closed-captioning/closed-captioning-requirements/

[21] www.google.com/url?q=https://www.w3.org/TR/webvtt1/

[22] https://journals.sagepub.com/doi/10.1177/2059799118790743

[23] https://docs.microsoft.com/en-us/azure/cognitive-services/speech-service/how-to-custom-speech-evaluate-data

Apart from availability of captions, giving users the option to adjust the size of captions ensures that people with overlapping hearing impairments and low vision can access the content. If the design and implementation account for different text size preferences, presenting captions in other languages that might take more screen space comes at no additional cost.

In the following, we see an example of captions presented with regular text size (Figure 3-16), followed by a screen with captions in large font (Figure 3-17). Lastly, we have a screen showing captions in German (Figure 3-18).

Figure 3-16. *Mobile screen with video and default size captions*

Figure 3-17. *Mobile screen with video and enlarged captions*

Figure 3-18. *Mobile screen with video and captions in German*

Sound Cues Alone Are Not Used to Convey Meaning

Visual or text alternatives for sound-based information should be present. For example, while playing an online game, if a user enters an erroneous command, a beep lets the user know they made an error. In this case, the game should also present a visual or text cue. On phones, haptic feedback is sometimes used to reinforce error messaging.

Beyond Compliance

The use cases for captions go well beyond accessibility. One video publisher with over 150 million users on Facebook reported that 85% of videos were watched without sound.[24] Captions also allow for search, intelligent segmentation, translation (and therefore broader reach), and smart features on top of media files that would not otherwise be possible. Potential use cases of transcripts and captions are discussed in further detail in the case study below.

Case Study: Transcripts and Captions

A few years ago, when I worked at Yahoo Finance, our team collaborated with the accessibility team on a project called "Live tickers." Closed captions on all prerecorded financial markets news already met the compliance requirement. We decided to go one step further.

In this project, we combined captions, machine learning, and front-end design to show the live stock price of companies that a reporter was talking about in real time as part of the video experience.

News providers in the financial markets sector already have this feature as you might have seen on tv, but it requires someone to manually identify and post this information. The automated solution is far more scalable and customizable. For example, it can pull in stock prices from when the news came out, and show its current price for comparison if the video is being watched later.

This was an example of assistive technology powering a richer experience for everyone. Another benefit of transcripts and captions is SEO or Search Engine Optimization. Discovery Digital Networks (DDN) performed an experiment on their YouTube channel, comparing videos with and without closed captions. They found that captioned videos enjoyed 7.32% more views on average.[25] Captions and transcripts also give way to creating subtitles that can open up content to entirely new demographics.

---

[24] https://instapage.com/blog/closed-captioning-mute-videos

[25] www.3playmedia.com/blog/7-ways-video-transcripts-captions-improve-seo/

Similar to the live ticker feature, captions enable search and navigation to specific parts of a media file. It can also power automatic semantic segmentation of videos into individual sections. For example, YouTube allows creators to add chapters to their videos so watchers can skip to segment-wise timestamps, as shown in Figure 3-19. Viewers can also share specific sections of the video.

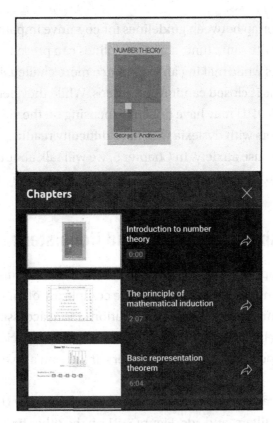

Figure 3-19. *Screenshot of a YouTube video on Number Theory with individual chapters' timestamps and share buttons under the video player*

Currently, the uploader decides where these breakpoints are. Captions combined with natural language processing might enable this feature by default, without manual segmentation, and even personalize sections for individual watchers.

Another amazing feature powered by live captions is live transcription and auto-generated meeting notes so people can focus on communication during meetings.

People with Cognitive Impairment

After motor impairments, this is the second most common form of disability. According to the CDC, over 16 million people in the United States live with cognitive impairments. Some examples of cognitive impairment are autism, attention deficit, dyslexia, dyscalculia, and memory loss.

There is a lot of overlap between guidelines for cognitive impairments and other types of disabilities. At the same time, some guidelines can present conflicts, that is, they help one group of users while making an experience more challenging for another group.

One example of this is closed captions on videos. While they help users with hearing loss, some users with ADHD may have difficulty focusing on the video while there is text on the screen.[26] For users with dyslexia who have difficulty reading, additional text on the screen might also cause anxiety. In Chapter 5, we will talk about personalization so users have the ability to choose fonts and other parts of the experience they feel most comfortable with.

Content Is Organized, Digestible, and Consistent

Adding features to an application is the easiest thing for teams to do. The less intuitive thing to do is to constantly evaluate the cognitive complexity of functionality on a given app or screen. This not only makes applications more accessible for people with cognitive impairments but also more intuitive for everyone. Especially on mobile, where the number of UI components and actions a user can take on a given screen is limited to begin with.

Figure 3-20 is an example of a mobile interface with too many UI components including a search bar, filters, and ads. Figure 3-21 on the other hand shows a simpler interface with a focus on search results.

---

[26] http://davidlewisphd.com/publications/2012-AECT-LewisBrown.pdf

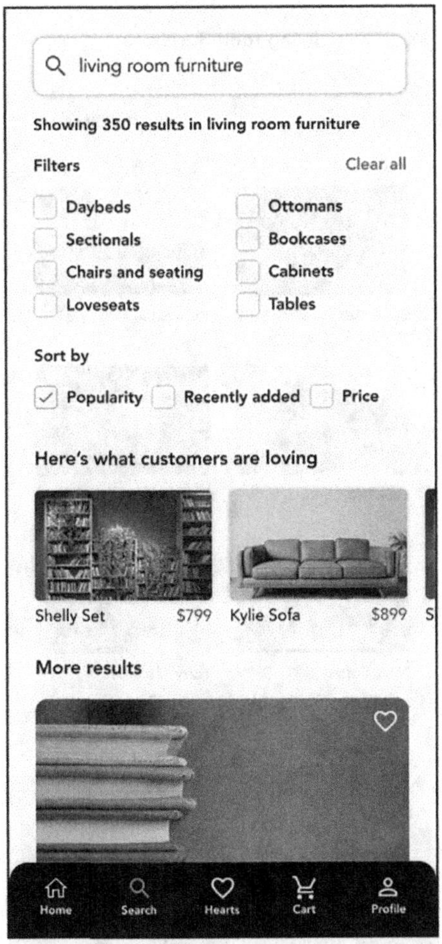

Figure 3-20. *Mobile screen with a lot of content – search box, filters, and sorting options with checkboxes, recommendations*

Figure 3-21. *Mobile screen with filters and sorting options in a more digestible format*

Timeouts or Limits on Interactions Are Adjustable

If an interaction requires to be completed within a certain time frame, a user is given enough warning (20 seconds according to WCAG guidelines) before the expiration, or the ability to stop or adjust the timing. This especially applies to forms and other input activities where users can lose data if they are unable to complete a time-based task. These controls give users with reading or learning disabilities, as well as those with less experience with technology products sufficient time to complete tasks.

The exception to this rule is situations where real-time interaction is required, for example in real-time auctions.

Animations, Complex Language, and Auto-updating Content Can Be Turned Off or Paused

Animations, flashing visuals, and auto-updating content can create an engaging user experience for some audiences. People prone to seizures, anxiety, and other cognitive disabilities, however, may have an adverse reaction to these interactions. Web developers can disable these interactions if the user has declared their preference accessible via media query as shown in the following code sample:[27]

```
@media (prefers-reduced-motion: reduce) {
 button {
  animation: none;
 }
}
```

For mobile developers, using the operating system's standard APIs for animations is the easiest way to ensure that user preferences on disabling or slow animation are honored.

Instructions and Errors on Forms Are Presented as Text, and in Context

For example, if a user needs to input a date in MM-DD-YYYY format, that is part of the instructions next to the field. The user is then less likely to fill an entire form, and at the submission stage come back to a list of errors that could have been avoided with clear instructions.

Below we have two sets of images that show common pitfalls in online forms and side-by-side comparisons with remediation for those pitfalls.

---

[27] https://web.dev/prefers-reduced-motion

The first set of images (Figure 3-22) shows a payment form where the field name, such as card number, disappears as soon as a user starts typing, which can be confusing and disorienting for people with short memory or attention spans. Next to this image is an example of the field remaining visible at all times.

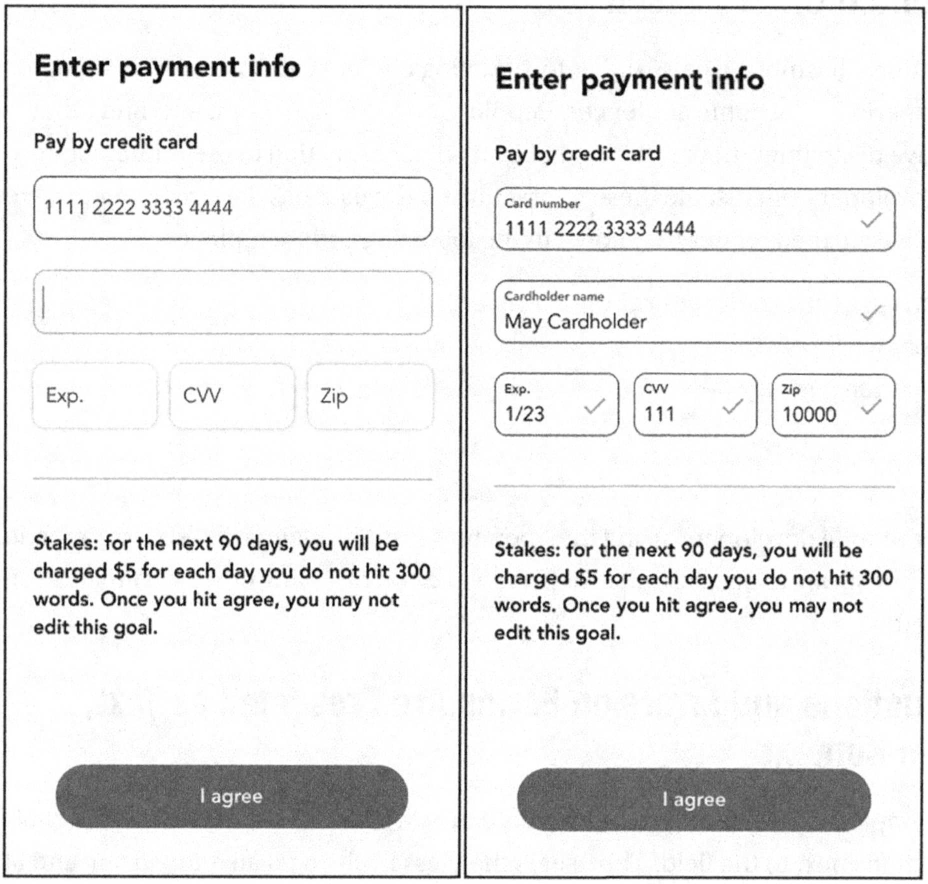

Figure 3-22. *Side-by-side comparison of two payment screens. On the left, is a screenshot of a credit card payment screen where the hint "cardholder name" disappears upon focus. On the right, is a screenshot of a credit card payment screen with the hint "cardholder name" visible as the user types*

In the next set (Figure 3-23), we have an example screenshot where all errors related to a form are reported above the form. This is even more concerning in longer forms, which might require users to scroll through multiple pages in order to correct their input and verify the new input. For people with anxiety, memory, attention, and other cognitive impairments, it can be overwhelming to fill out a simple form if error messaging and remediation instructions are not in context.

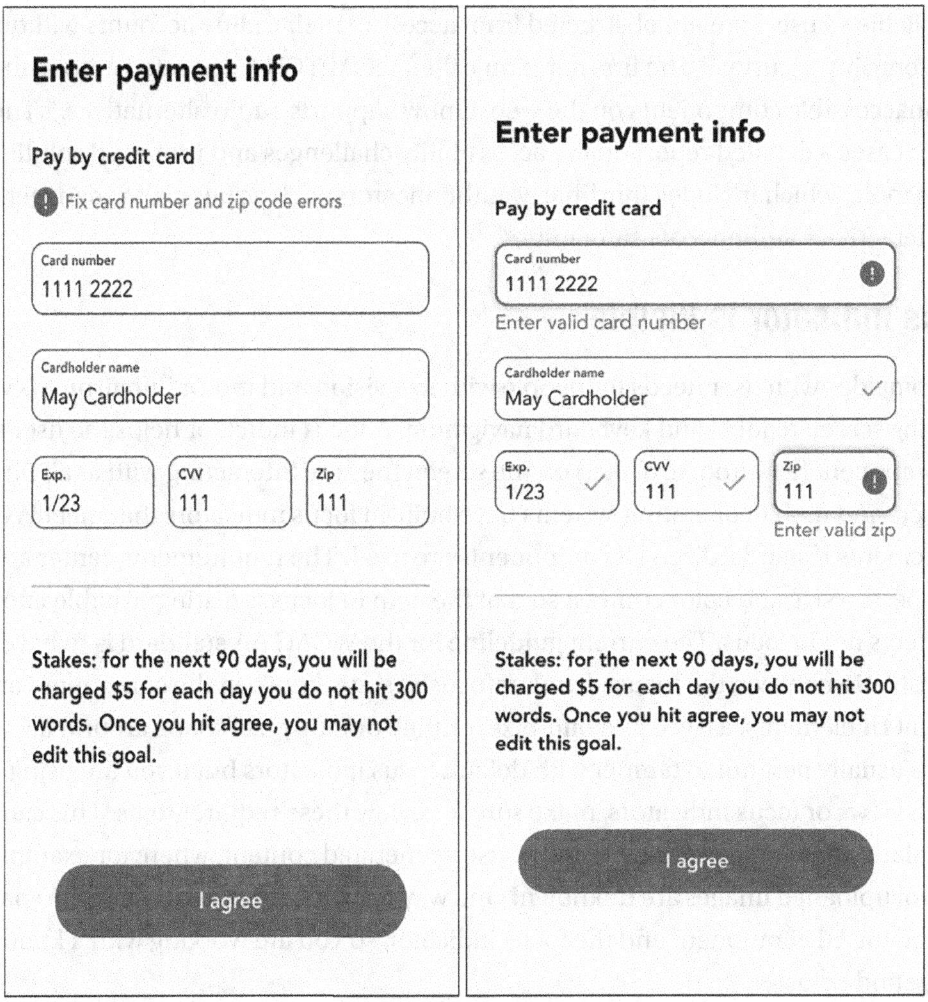

Figure 3-23. *Two screenshots of error reporting on a credit card form. On the left, is a screenshot of a credit card payment screen with all errors appearing together on top. On the right, a screenshot of a credit card payment screen with errors appearing next to the field with error*

Next to the first image is an example with the error message appearing below the field in question, which updates dynamically as the user enters new information, instead of waiting for form submission.

Captcha and Other Authentication Methods Have Alternatives

This overlaps with user needs for people with visual impairments. Audio Captcha, two-factor authentication, or alternate ways of verifying identity as a human must be available so users are not obstructed from access to their online accounts without compromising security.[28] The first iteration called reCAPTCHA was rated among the most inaccessible components on the web. It now supports audio alternatives.[29] The W3C releases a detailed report on the accessibility challenges and proposed solutions on this topic, which includes third-party authenticators such as password managers to noninteractively authenticate humanity.[30]

Focus Indicator Is Visible

This coincides with user needs for people with low vision and motor impairments who are using screen readers and keyboard navigation. A focus indicator helps the user know the component (a button, text, etc.) on the screen they are interacting with at all times. Browsers and mobile operating systems have built-in focus indicators that meet WCAG requirements if standardized UI components are used. The requirements center around two aspects – size and color contrast so that the item in focus is distinguishable enough from items not in focus. The current guideline for the WCAG AA standard is to have a 3:1 contrast ratio between the focused and unfocused state, between the component and its adjacent UI elements, as well as a one-pixel outline or four-pixel shape around it.[31]

It is usually best not to tamper with default focus indicators but if you are using custom views or focus indicators, make sure to review these requirements. This can be particularly challenging with dynamic or user-generated content, where for example, the colors of uploaded images are unknown. One way to tackle this is to leave some space between the UI component and the focus indicator, so you are working with a known background color.

---

[28] www.w3.org/TR/turingtest/#the-accessibility-challenge

[29] https://support.google.com/recaptcha/answer/6175971?hl=en

[30] www.w3.org/TR/turingtest/#fedtoken

[31] www.w3.org/WAI/WCAG21/Understanding/focus-visible.html

Beyond Compliance

Making content easily readable, less chaotic, and more understandable is simply good design and engineering practice. Simplifying user flows, and removing features is not only good for engagement and reach (creating a smaller application or web page size), but also better for teams to maintain.

People with Speech Impairment

Voice as a mode of interaction with our devices is growing significantly with developments in the IoT (Internet of Things) space with devices such as voice assistants. According to Google, 27% of the global population is already using voice search[32] on mobile. Voice-activated applications are vastly more accessible for people with visual and fine-motor impairments.

We need to make sure that we don't leave out other subsets of the population, such as people with speech and hearing impairments.

According to NIH[33] data, about 7.5 million people in the United States have trouble using their voice. For applications that move toward a voice-first approach, it will be important to still maintain alternate modalities of interaction that are visual or text-based.

Another reason to consider alternate modalities is that even within the voice domain, there is so much diversity in speech patterns and accents, even among able-bodied users, that providing alternatives is the only way to ensure that all users have access. ASR (Automatic Speech Recognition) is as good as 95% for native English speakers but significantly lower for non-native speakers. For less common speech patterns, accents or languages, that number can dramatically decrease. This is mainly because the data used to train the machine learning models for these situations is limited. Siri, the voice assistant on Apple devices famously had trouble understanding accents[34] when it first launched. Most voice assistants, including Siri[35] now allow users to pick their accents and languages, and train the assistant to understand unique speech patterns.

---

[32] www.dbswebsite.com/blog/trends-in-voice-search/

[33] www.nidcd.nih.gov/health/statistics/statistics-voice-speech-and-language

[34] www.fastcompany.com/1799374/siri-why-cant-you-understand-me

[35] https://support.apple.com/en-us/HT208316

Primarily Voice Input Applications Provide Alternative Ways of Interaction

The voice use case is not usually covered in guidelines due to its recent popularity and the fact that most actions that can be accomplished with voice also have alternate equivalents (keyboard or touch through visual interfaces).

Google's project Euphonia[36] is a great example of an artificial intelligence application in making speech technology more accessible to people with conditions such as ALS (amyotrophic lateral sclerosis) and Down syndrome. The technology trains on people's natural intonations and speech patterns during the early stages and helps them communicate with their own voice after they lose speech. It has also been used to trigger smart home devices using nonspeech sounds, as well as to cheer during a sports game using facial gestures on one user with ALS.[37] According to a 2021 study,[38] the technology is already outperforming human transcribers, especially for the most severely affected people.

Beyond Compliance

> Text alternatives to voice input can also provide a fallback for when the voice application doesn't have sufficient data to understand uncommon accents and speech patterns.

> Voice command features on mobile sometimes rely on accessibility labels, demonstrating yet another case where solving for one use case opens the door to several others.

People with Mobility Impairment

17% of the US population suffers from some form of mobility impairment.[39] Examples include muscular dystrophy, multiple sclerosis, ALS, Parkinson's disease, and essential tremor.

---

[36] https://sites.research.google/euphonia/

[37] https://ai.googleblog.com/2021/08/recreating-natural-voices-for-people.html

[38] www.isca-speech.org/archive/pdfs/interspeech_2021/green21_interspeech.pdf

[39] www.cdc.gov/ncbddd/disabilityandhealth/infographic-disability-impacts-all.html

These conditions can make using touch-screen interfaces, keyboards, and mice difficult. Assistive technologies for users with dexterity limitations include sip and puff sticks, single-switch access, adaptive keyboards, and eye or head-tracking software. Now let's talk about guidelines that can make applications inclusive for these users:

All Content Is Accessible Through a Keyboard

This especially applies to mobile and touchscreen devices, with which users attach external keyboards or custom assistive devices. The most rudimentary way to check whether an application is largely keyboard accessible is to pair a keyboard with the device, and navigate through the content (this is done by using the "Tab" key). This also ties in with the guideline on meaningful grouping and focus order we covered in the section on visual impairments and screen readers, where users can navigate by headings instead of tabbing through every element on a page. Additionally, for speech input users, as well as keyboard users who might not be able to type accurately, a user should be able to turn off or remap character key shortcuts.

All actions should be available without requiring timing or individual keystrokes. This is important for users with specialized or adapted input devices such as a head pointer, eye-gaze system, or speech-controlled mouse emulator, which makes certain gestures cumbersome, error-prone, or outright impossible.[40] One example of this is a sortable list that requires a user to drag and drop items precisely in the position they want.

While drag and drop is a great interactive way to place elements where a user wants them, developers must also provide a way for users to reorder elements individually. For example, by entering the item's place in the list, or moving an item up and down, one at a time.

Motion Actuation, Pointer Focus, or Activation Is Reversible

A user is able to remove focus from an element that can receive keyboard focus. The same applies to the activation of functions upon clicking or by certain movements of the device. For example, some apps allow activation of functions when a user shakes the device. This might happen unintentionally for users with motor impairments, or

---

[40] www.w3.org/WAI/WCAG22/Understanding/dragging-movements

for anyone, and the user should be able to either turn off the functionality or be able to reverse it when it happens. Equally, these applications can't rely on the idea that a user will be able to shake the device at all, as the device may be mounted to a wheelchair or other assistive device.

Beyond Compliance

Providing keyboard access goes hand in hand with screen-reader access and focus order. Elements that are accessible by keyboard are also accessible to screen readers.

Everyone

Here are the guidelines that apply to everyone, whether or not they use assistive technology:

Avoid Using Jargon or Unnecessarily Complicated Language

There are tests such as the Flesch-Kincaid reading test,[41] that you can run through text to ensure that the content isn't too difficult to read for your target audience. This is particularly important for marketing material or user onboarding messaging.

Adhere to Global Settings

We have touched on this in the previous sections on text sizes, animation settings, color inversion, and dark mode. If users have accessibility settings enabled on their device, developers must honor those settings within the application's context. Similarly, if the user has chosen an in-app custom accessibility setting, it is a better user experience to persist (save) those settings between sessions, so the user does not have to reconfigure them everytime.

---

[41] www.textcompare.org/readability/flesch-kincaid-grade-level/

Allow Users to Provide Feedback

User feedback is a goldmine of possible improvements to their existing offering, as well as new ways to serve their customers. The best product teams make it as easy and intuitive as possible for users to provide their feedback. Having multiple channels such as email, phone, and live chat that meet a variety of functional needs is crucial for people with disabilities. This also allows all users to engage with customer support teams in the way they prefer. An example of this is shown in Figure 3-24.

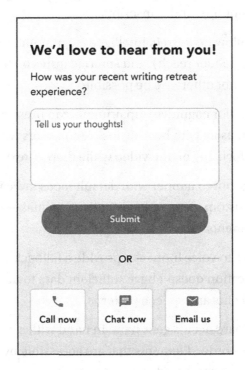

Figure 3-24. *Screenshot of a feedback screen with options to call, chat, or email*

Summary

- The most common type of assistive technology used by people with complete or partial blindness is screen readers. For people with color blindness or light sensitivity, settings such as dark mode, brightness, or color inversion are other forms of assistive technology.

- Screen readers use the alternative text provided by the website or application to read to the user when they focus on a component.

- If the content is user generated the product can encourage content creators to add description text as part of the captions section at the upload stage, or use image recognition to provide labels for images that don't have captions.

- Links should also be visually distinguishable from regular text and with text that describes what the link is.

- Assistive technology used by people with hearing loss includes hearing aids, captions, and transcripts.

- Captions also allow for search, intelligent segmentation, translation (and therefore broader reach), and smart features on top of media files that would not otherwise be possible.

- Some guidelines for cognitive impairments can present conflicts. While they help users with hearing loss, some users with ADHD may have difficulty focusing on the video while there is text on the screen.

- It is usually best not to tamper with default focus indicators but if you are using custom views or focus indicators, make sure to review WCAG requirements.

- Text alternatives to voice input can provide a fallback for when the voice application doesn't have sufficient data to understand uncommon accents and speech patterns.

- Providing keyboard access goes hand in hand with screen-reader access and focus order. Elements that are accessible by keyboard are also accessible to screen readers.

- A broader definition of accessibility would include avoiding complicated language, adhering to global settings, and allowing users to provide feedback.

CHAPTER 4

Gameplan

In the last chapter, we covered user needs based on types of disabilities, and the reach of corresponding solutions beyond accessibility. First, for those working on existing products and features, we will talk about ways to address current issues. Second, we will talk about integrating the solutions discussed in Chapter 3 into the software development lifecycle so we can eliminate the need for large audits and short-term solutions.

Addressing Existing Issues

Existing issues come from either customer reports, audits, or legal complaints. Digital accessibility encompasses an extremely complex set of problems, which at first can be overwhelming.

If a large product has mostly been built without accessibility in mind, the first complete audit report can seem like an insurmountable amount of work. The first thing to understand is that it's okay to not get everything right at once. The second is to realize that a majority of these issues are easily fixable. We just need a systematic framework to assign priority and responsibilities across the team to move through the findings.

Audits are a great way to get a holistic view of which parts of the experience work, and which need work. In big, distributed teams, another benefit of thorough audits is that products are evaluated from the perspective of a user, instead of how their implementation happens to be divided among teams. Having a consolidated view of issues also uncovers opportunities for education and centralization of core components that can be reused with accessibility built-in.

Once you have an audit report, approaching teams with all of the issues at once is a recipe for not getting anything done. Another common pitfall when approaching teams is to lead with compliance and legal requirements instead of educating them on the business value of accessible products, with an awareness of the compliance aspect. The first approach is likely to kill the desire for innovation because the goal is to tick a compliance box, while the other encourages the team to think creatively. Whether it is a consultant, a central accessibility team, or your own development team, the most effective way of driving change is to take a tiered approach. The steps are outlined here.

1.   Is this part of a key user flow?

You will need to work with a product manager, designer, or engineer on the team to understand which user flows are the most critical, for users and for the business. An example of a core user flow of a new application is the signup process, which prevents users from doing anything else on the application.

Minor issue on a major flow ➤ Major issue on a fringe user flow

2.   Is the issue a blocker? Is there an alternative way for users to complete the flow?

Accessibility issues can be blockers, that is, an assistive technology user is prevented from moving forward in a flow. If so, this needs to be prioritized above other issues in key user flows. A classic example of this is when the focus sequence is broken, and a user is trapped in a certain section of the page.

3.   What is the level of effort required to fix this issue?

Fixing can mean different things depending on the goal. Is it:

(a).   To meet requirements

(b).   To do better than meeting requirements (seriously, do better)

(c).   An innovative industry-leading user experience (the space is ripe for innovation)

To determine the ease of implementation, a useful way to break down existing issues is to separate the ones that require visual design changes and those that do not. If the design does not change visually, there are way fewer steps involved in implementation and validation. Table 4-1 shows all the items from Chapter 3, separated by whether they need a visual design refresh.

Table 4-1. *Accessibility considerations that require visual design change vs. not*

No visual design change	Requires visual design change
Content labels (alt-text)	Dynamic sizing
Headings	Visual only cues
Meaningful focus sequence	Link indicators
Link descriptions	Audio description
Auto-playing volume off	Captions and transcripts
Adjustable timeouts	Text alternatives to sound cues
Keyboard accessibility	Organized, digestible content
Reversible keyboard focus	Configurable animations
	Form instructions and errors
	Captcha and authentication alternatives
	Alternative for voice interaction
	Help and feedback channels

4. Are there systemic issues that are better addressed with common components?

This is one of the best uses of an extensive audit. If you see similar gaps in different parts of an application, it is a great opportunity to

- Consolidate components into central libraries

- Identify teams that can benefit from accessibility education

- Add automated and manual checks

Getting teams to centralize and adopt components is a more long-term effort, which is why this is the last item on the list. Finding local fixes while working on centralizing components might involve some duplicate work, but unblocking users will in most cases be worth it.

The Software Product Lifecycle: Embedding Inclusion

Software development, much like the products that come out of it, is about people. Most accessibility conversations focus on the design aspects and have a built-in assumption that products designed with inclusion in mind will continue to be inclusive. Design is only one part of the process, and this view places a disproportionate burden on design for what is everyone's responsibility.

We cannot solve the problem holistically unless we take into account each actor involved in the development process, their responsibilities, and how accessibility fits into their roles.

Let's illustrate this with an example. Imagine we are building a new onboarding flow that includes allowing users to sign in to our application using a third-party authentication service. It has the screens shown in Figure 4-1, Figure 4-2, and Figure 4-3.

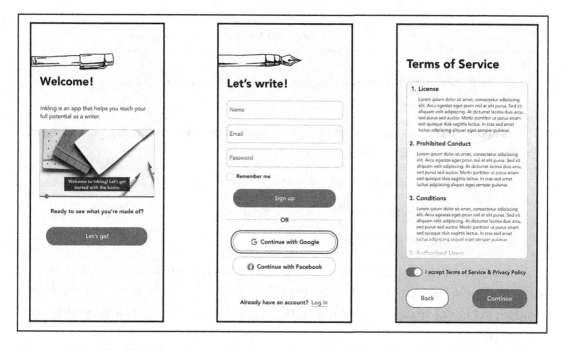

Figure 4-1. *The first three screens in an onboarding flow. Screen 1 – Video preview with captions on the main features of the app. Screen 2 – Login or Sign up page with options to link existing accounts. Screen 3 – Terms of service page with a toggle to agree*

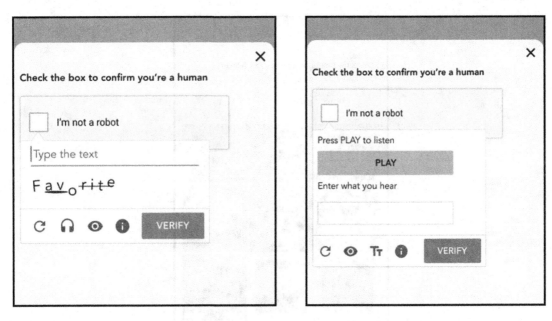

Figure 4-2. *The screenshot on the left shows a Captcha screen with text. The screenshot on the right shows a Captcha screen with audio*

Figure 4-3. *Mobile screenshot showing a grid of images to identify*

Now, let's deep dive into the actors involved, and where they fit from an accessibility perspective. These responsibilities apply regardless of agile,[1] waterfall,[2] or other project management methodologies.

Product Management

As a product manager, you are ultimately responsible for what is shipped to customers. In other words, the buck stops with you.

In this example, you would be responsible for the following:

---

[1] www.agilealliance.org/agile101/

[2] www.umsl.edu/~hugheyd/is6840/waterfall.html

1. Vetting third parties used in the flow for their accessibility practices and statements

2. When writing user stories, going through the user needs we covered in Chapter 3 (or your own list) to make sure at least the basics are covered

3. Following up on other team members' priorities

4. Defining and communicating about user flows that are most critical to the user and the business, so when issues come up, they are prioritized correctly

5. Defining cohorts of users by their unique needs

6. Measuring success and identifying bottlenecks for each cohort in further iterations

7. Identifying areas where automated and manual testing should become part of the release or sign-off process

User Research and Insights

This includes both qualitative and quantitative methods of gathering data and validating the direction as well as the implementation of product features. In other words, generative and evaluative studies.

User researchers make sure people with disabilities are represented in qualitative studies, surveys, and other research methods. It will not be possible to cover every use case, but having representation from as many groups as possible ensures that the experience is not designed for a homogenous audience, or solely through the lens of designers and developers.

Setting up equipment, especially remotely requires training and experience with assistive technologies that user researcher programs commonly don't teach.

As mentioned in Chapter 2 in the section on measuring impact qualitatively, there are companies that specialize in conducting usability studies with assistive technology users, in-person and remotely. While not a replacement for in-person interviews, remote studies present an opportunity to expand the reachable user base and to allow research in users' natural settings. For example, the NHS in the UK found that it was more efficient to recruit study participants who could previously not travel for in-person studies because of disabilities or geographic barriers.[3]

For smaller businesses, it might not be feasible to afford the associated cost of hiring user researchers who specialize in studying assistive technology or contracting another company. In that situation, relying on direct user feedback, visiting an empathy lab, or putting yourself in your users' shoes by trying your application under different circumstances can provide invaluable insights.

When selecting vendors for studies, and survey tools, researchers must either ensure that their tools are accessible to the intended participants or work with procurement to read their VPAT (Voluntary Product Accessibility Template).

On the quantitative side, data science and user insights teams will work on instrumentation (sending events for specific user interactions) and identification of key markers of engagement. Geographic location, local regulations, and platform will determine the types of data that can be collected and the limitations on processing it.

Before conducting research with real users, it is vital to ask the following questions:

1. Have we done a common-sense pass on the product to ensure we at least have the basics covered?

2. Have we confirmed with a range of people with lived experience that they can reasonably use this product?

3. If not, can we engage people with lived experience to build something they can easily use?

Project Management

The multidisciplinary problem-solving required to build accessible applications and websites necessitates collaboration and communication between various stakeholders. Project managers make sure that the specific teams involved, and stakeholders are on the same page about priorities, timelines, dependencies, and blockers. For this reason, product and project managers are usually in the best position to be "accessibility champions" for businesses trying to improve their companies' approach, as they communicate with so many different disciplines and keep a holistic view of the product.

---

[3] https://digital.nhs.uk/blog/design-matters/2021/going-remote-how-we-adapted-our-accessibility-research

Design

Design principles for accessibility compliance are heavily documented in current literature. Most design guidelines tend to be at a component level, while design encompasses both components and how they behave together, that is, interaction design. Chapter 3 covered component-level design considerations in depth. The following principles apply at a more holistic level to designing for accessibility.

Creativity and Common Sense Before Rules

As demonstrated in the case study in Chapter 1 on accessible data visualization, starting from user needs and first principles is sometimes better than following existing rules. Before wholesale adopting the status quo, designers have the opportunity to employ their creative strengths and deep knowledge of their products to create truly exceptional user experiences.

When in Doubt, Use Standard Patterns

For custom UI components and interactions, you will need to come up with new accessibility patterns. For common UI interactions, unless the intent is to enhance its functionality and accessibility of it, it is better to stick with system defaults and accepted paradigms. This is because users are accustomed to design patterns on their respective devices and unless learning a new pattern benefits their experience, it is just unnecessary overhead. Native components also usually have accessibility built-in, so developers don't have to worry about accessibility at the component level, and can instead focus on how different components work together.

For example, a common mobile pattern is to have tabs at the bottom of the screen for easy navigation. If a new design were to propose these be located at the top or on the right/left edge of the screen, there should be a compelling reason besides it looking cool.

Avoid Custom Experiences Based on Assistive Technology Use

Operating systems will sometimes let an application detect whether assistive technology is in use. Although designing a parallel, custom experience for use with assistive technology might seem like a great idea at first, it should only be considered when it is not possible to make the primary experience equally accessible, or when the custom experience has clear benefits to users with the specific assistive technology. If a custom experience is available, users without the assistive technology setting should be able to access it, and those with the setting should be able to turn it off.

There are a few reasons for this

1. Not all assistive technologies are detected. External hardware and third-party plug-ins might not be detectable by applications, or their detection might be restricted due to privacy regulations.

2. Building and maintaining parallel experiences is expensive and time-consuming for the development team.

Consider the Broadest Possible Use Case

Below are a few questions to help get you started on thinking through different scenarios:

If we offered this in every language, how would the interface need to adapt?

If we inverted colors, are there components such as videos that should be left as is?

If I couldn't view any of the colors on this page, would I still be able to interact with it?

If I only had text labels (no images or symbols), how would this work?

If I could do just one thing on this screen, what would it be? What about 2?

If I had an old, small device, how would this work?

What happens when there is a network failure?

What about a notification?

What about error states?

Are we making assumptions about the user's context? What if they aren't true?

Handle Loading States Effectively

While it is good practice to let users know when they are waiting for a screen to load on all platforms, it is especially important on mobile. Only one (and in some cases two) applications can be in the foreground (visibly running on the screen) at any given time, which also determines how network and hardware resources are allocated. For users with disabilities, if the progress is not accurately reflected, it might cause them to be confused, or worse, abandon the process altogether. Having a progress indicator is considered universal good practice, since slow or unresponsive applications can cause as many as 60% of users to abandon the experience altogether.[4]

Don't Overuse Modals, Tooltips, and Popups

Modals (dialog box on top of a page), tooltips, and popups are commonly used to draw the user's attention to a specific part of the page or to prompt an action. Use cases include payment flows from third parties, error dialogs, and help text that appears on hover/click. Accessibility challenges with these elements are:

1. Cognitive overload if overused

2. Covering part of the content on page

3. Keyboard traps if not handled correctly

Accessibility Never Gets in the Way of Good Design

Good design *is* accessible. Designers not familiar with the accessibility principles and patterns might push back on accessible design in favor of what might seem more visually appealing. Below are two examples, one that might look more minimalistic and aesthetically pleasing to someone without vision loss or color blindness (Figure 4-4) and one that is more accessible (Figure 4-5). Remember, there is always a way to make beautiful interfaces that work for *everyone*.

---

[4]www.appdynamics.com/media/uploaded-files/mobileapp.pdf

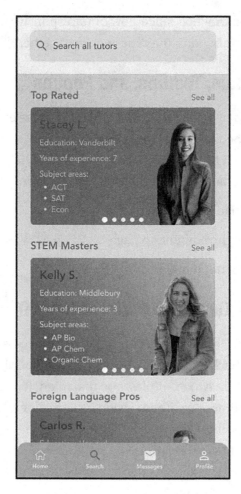

Figure 4-4. *Mobile screen with a limited color palette that to an unfamiliar eye, might be mistaken for minimalist and aesthetically pleasing*

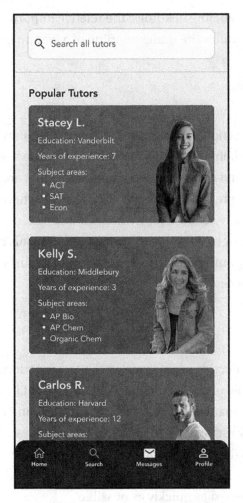

Figure 4-5. *Mobile screen with the same content as the one before except it has sufficient color contrast*

Multiple Use Cases Represented in Deliverables

When a designer gives files or specs to the development team for implementation, different use cases that consider the questions above should be represented in those deliverables. Not only do they set expectations for engineers so they don't have to refactor code later on, they can also be used as a foundation for quality assurance scripts or behavior-based testing, if that's part of the team's process.

Furthermore, clearly labeling headings, the relative importance of components, and focus order on a page solidifies the understanding of a feature across product, design, and engineering.

Design Plugins

This one sits at the intersection of design and engineering. Many design tools come with accessibility plugins that help test things such as color contrast, item labels, etc. Using a consistent color palette, and central design components that are built with accessibility, frees up time for larger, more complex issues such as interaction design.

Design tools can already account for dynamic user flows, multiple states, device sizes, and contingencies for realistic prototyping. As these tools become more sophisticated, combining automated checks at this level to surface gaps can further streamline the accessible development cycle.

Engineering

Inclusive design is only effective when translated into a functional application at the engineering stage. The role of a great engineering team is not just implementing designs, but being an active participant in the discovery, validation, and design process.

Engineers are in the best position to identify opportunities afforded by new software versions, tools, and changing industry practices. They are also responsible for writing automated tests, and building ways for the test results to flow back to designers on their teams so issues are addressed as quickly as possible.

Engineers can also take up the more ambitious task of building bespoke design plugins to push the discovery of gaps upstream with design.

When in Doubt, Use System Defaults

If engineers notice a deviation from operating system defaults and accepted patterns, they will ask for justification. Not only is sticking with defaults better for the user (as discussed in the design section above), but also requires less code maintenance for the team.

Engineering Practices

Engineering teams will often follow best practices around test coverage, code quality, and testing paradigms. Incorporating accessibility testing in the local developer environment and team workflow, as well as in CI (continuous integration) saves a lot of time down the road. A few specific items to work on are as follows:

1. Platformization of design/UI components – Identify duplicate or similar UI elements and replace them with central components that have accessibility built-in

2. Add consistent linters to each developer's IDE (integrated development environments) so they are alerted on central UI components, as well as best practices in real time as they are coding

3. Write automated tests to cover at least key user flows that run either in the local development environment or in CI as part of the code review and merge process

4. As far as possible, make expandable views that have localized strings (text in different languages) or variable length content

Customer Experience

The customer experience team will work closely with product managers on onboarding, help pages, and FAQ (frequently asked questions) documentation for existing and new features, especially for use with assistive technology. The role of customer experience teams is discussed in more detail in Chapter 6.

Marketing

In theory, the principles here are no different from the ones covered in product, design, and engineering above. The key difference is that the marketing team's work spans beyond the core product offering, and can be easy to overlook. This includes promotional material, banners, adverts, and partnerships with other products, companies, and channels the core team has little control over.

Even if marketing material is not part of the core offering, it is still very much part of the brand, and how a lot of first-time customers will learn of the product.

Specific items marketing teams are responsible for the following:

- Vetting third-party marketing channels for inclusive practices

- Highlighting accessibility features as part of onboarding

Here are some quick tips:

- Camelcase hashtags so screen readers can identify individual words. For example, #ThisIsTheBestProductEver is a more accessible hashtag than #thissisthebestproductever

- Run marketing campaigns, especially static pages through an accessibility scanner

- Use inclusive language in emails, landing pages, surveys, and other channels

Testing

Automated and manual testing is discussed in further detail in Chapter 6.

Procurement

Adding VPATs (Voluntary Product Accessibility Template) to the evaluation and procurement criteria for SaaS vendors is one way to ensure that product facets not developed in-house meet at least common guidelines. Teams can have their own requirements on top of that, but this ensures a good baseline level of accessibility.

Leadership and Business Stakeholders

Your attitude toward inclusion and accessibility will dictate how the rest of the company values it. Understanding that investing slightly more time in getting it right the first time is less expensive than having to fix it later, and way less expensive than a lawsuit will go a long way.

In the case of companies that have longstanding products and are starting to think about accessibility, leadership will be responsible for setting the right tone and putting subject matter experts in place. Teach Access, for example, is a nonprofit that brings industry experts, academics, and advocates as great resources on what to look for in various accessibility specialist roles.

Technology leaders, similar to a majority of their teams, will likely not be subject matter experts. Realizing that inexperience can be an advantage is one of the most powerful ideas that executives can embrace, and lead by example. Instead of implementing the status quo, they can focus on what is possible and bring in fresh ideas. Subject matter experts should of course be part of the picture to make sure there aren't obvious gaps, but not having subject matter expertise should not be a valid excuse for inaction.

Compliance is rarely the thing that gets people excited about doing work. If leaders take a keen interest in inclusion and innovation, they can build the momentum product teams need to truly understand all customer needs. Some ways to kick off a celebration of diversity, instead of a checklist are

1. Holding a hackathon centered around accessibility

2. Adding accountability through performance reviews and hiring criteria

While the above initiatives are great to build momentum, for sustainable change, accessibility needs to be part of company OKRs (Objectives and Key Results), promotion criteria, and how teams and evaluated.

Legal, Privacy, and Security

The intersection of security and accessibility calls for special attention because ignoring one comes at the expense of the other. For example, if the user flow above contains a Captcha screen that requires a user to identify letters or objects in a grid of images, a visually impaired user may not be able to complete the challenge and prove they are human. Providing an audio Captcha method is one alternative. For deafblind users, neither of these methods works, so a system that works with a braille display might be the best option.

Another interesting challenge arises when users are asked or shown sensitive information on a screen. Both iOS and Android devices have privacy modes so users can make the screen go dark. If they have a screen reader on, the user should be asked before reading out sensitive data. These are some of the same considerations that would apply to a car app or a voice assistant-based product.

Accessibility Team or Consultants

Ideally, the accessibility team has already done its work to educate and empower individual teams on each of their roles and responsibilities. The accessibility team's charter would be to step in as consultants on things the team might have missed, audit arrangements, and innovation in making the experience even better. The upfront work to educate and empower teams includes:

Education and Evangelism

Since baseline knowledge of accessibility and inclusion in technology is not part of most college or professional curricula, the accessibility team is responsible for onboarding new hires, and working with existing teams on

- Documentation of responsibilities based on roles

- How to use assistive technology for testing

- Engaging with real users

- Fine-tuning product development workflows

- Frequency and depth of audits

Community

There is an incredible community of industry experts, academics, and researchers who work on problems concerning more than one product or company. Organizations such as W3C (the World Wide Web Consortium), the American Association of People with Disabilities, the United Nations CRPD and Teach Access work on different aspects of advocacy, education, and guidelines. There are also advocacy groups such as the American Foundation for the Blind at the national level, and various others at state and local levels that can prove to be great partners for product development teams.

Apart from directly engaging with these organizations, digital accessibility conferences are great avenues for exchanging ideas and learning. CSUN (California State University, Northridge) conference, Web4All, AxeCon, and GAAD (Global Accessibility Awareness Day) are some of the more prominent ones. Specialized conferences are excellent at advancing the field among subject matter experts. The trend of inclusion as a central topic at mainstream technology conferences such as Google I/O, WWDC, CES (Consumer Electronics Show), etc., is particularly exciting because it opens up the problem space to everyone involved in product development, and identifies it as a key area to a global audience.

Innovation

Arguably the most important role of the accessibility team is to engage with the disability and academic community to constantly question the status quo, and push the boundaries of what it means to be inclusive. One effective way of doing this is to have subject matter experts embedded with specific feature teams and vice versa. One brings nuanced knowledge of the product and how it is engineered, while the other brings a nuanced perspective on how users with disabilities might be better served.

Accessibility Champions/Ambassadors

In companies early in their accessibility journeys, it is common to identify individuals who independently advocate for inclusion within the scope of their roles or beyond. While recognizing those who are passionate about accessibility is a great way to encourage people, it can have unintended consequences. Similar to how a central accessibility team accountable for everything accessibility-related is counterproductive, placing the responsibility on a few ambassadors or champions can also be detrimental to promoting the idea that inclusion is a part of everyone's role. In the long term, it is more sustainable and productive to have basic accessibility requirements during performance evaluations and promotions and to recognize and reward individuals who go above and beyond in product and/or process innovation in the area.

When Are We Done?

Stakeholders, executives, or other decision-makers might ask "So when can we call this done?" The answer is, when we stop developing or offering the product.

This is not to say that teams should not have milestones and deliverables. It means just as a world-class product evolves with time, the way it embraces inclusion should as well.

We can be done checking compliance boxes and doing audits, but we can't stop working on ways to make our products more inclusive.

Summary

- Audits are a great way to get a holistic view of which parts of the experience work, and which need work. In big, distributed teams, another benefit of thorough audits is that products are evaluated from the perspective of a user, instead of how their implementation happens to be divided among teams.

- Once you have an audit report, the most effective way of driving change is to take a tiered approach:

  - Is it part of a key user flow? Minor issues on a major flow should be prioritized over a major issue on a fringe user flow.

  - Is the issue a blocker? If so, prioritize it over Step 1.

  - Separate the required change into "no visual design change" and "requires visual design change." Addressing the latter will likely take less time.

  - Ask if these are systemic issues better addressed with common components.

- Most accessibility conversations place a disproportionate responsibility on designers, but the problem is best thought of holistically.

  - As a product manager, the buck stops with you.

- User researchers make sure that the experience is not designed for a homogenous audience, or solely through the lens of designers and developers.

- Product and project managers are usually in the best position to be "accessibility champions" for businesses trying to improve their companies' approach, as they communicate with so many different disciplines.

- When it comes to accessible design, starting from user needs and first principles is often better than following existing rules.

  - When in doubt, use standard patterns so as not to needlessly confuse user expectations.

  - Avoid custom experiences (not all assistive technology can be detected by the application and maintaining this parallel experience is time-consuming).

- A great engineering team does not just implement designs, but is an active participant in the discovery, validation, and design process.

  - Incorporating accessibility testing in the local developer environment and team workflow, as well as in CI (continuous integration) saves a lot of time down the road.

- Marketing teams are responsible for vetting third-party channels for inclusive practices and highlighting accessibility features as part of onboarding and procurement.

- Leadership is responsible for setting the right tone and putting subject matter experts in place. If leaders take a keen interest in inclusion and innovation, they will build the momentum product teams need.

- The accessibility team's charter would be to step in as consultants on things the team might have missed, audit arrangements, and innovation in making the experience even better.

CHAPTER 5

Nuances of Mobile Accessibility

In Chapter 1, we talked about the significance of mobile as a platform, and what makes mobile accessibility tricky. This chapter will cover the main challenges, and ways to address them.

Limited Documentation and Guidelines

Web accessibility guidelines, and design and implementation techniques, are extensively covered in current literature. The WCAG 2.0 standards that form the basis of most regulations were released in 2008. Mobile mapping for WCAG 2.0 was last published in 2015, for a set of guidelines written five years before that. In some regions such as the EU, WCAG 2.1 (released in 2018) has been an official recommendation since 2018 September 2021 was the first deadline for EU member states to report to the European Commission on their compliance with WCAG 2.1 at Level AA.

While web accessibility principles and fundamentals apply to all devices, they miss mobile-specific challenges. This is key given that we now live in a mobile-first world where 72% of all Internet users are estimated to solely use their mobile devices to access the web by 2025.[1]

The rapidly evolving mobile space has outpaced the documentation and adoption of these guidelines. With WCAG 3 underway, we will get closer to a more future-proof outcomes-based approach for platforms including mobile. What do we do in the meantime?

---

[1] Predicted by World Advertising Research Center

© Sukriti Chadha 2023
S. Chadha, *Beyond Accessibility Compliance*, https://doi.org/10.1007/978-1-4842-7948-9_5

Product teams could rely on platform-specific documentation for the Android[2] and iOS[3] accessibility.

However, as discussed before, guidelines are just baseline requirements. Talk to your users, and understand their needs and how they use your products. It will produce better outcomes than any set of guidelines.

Fragmentation

The term *Mobile* includes phones, tablets, wearables, and some IoT (Internet of Things) devices, with smartphones being the most prominent.

Even if we just consider phones, we need to account for mobile web (websites running on phone browsers), widgets, and mobile applications. Then there are the two most common operating systems, Android and iOS, that are completely different in terms of user experience, design paradigms, and tooling. The next level of fragmentation comes from all the different screen sizes, device configurations, and OS versions in the market. Designing a consistent brand experience that respects the integrity of the operating system across these individual devices is one of the factors that differentiates great products from good ones.

Between iOS and Android, there are different accessibility settings that introduce an added layer of complexity to the already fragmented mobile ecosystem. For example, on iOS, the screen reader (VoiceOver) uses a rotor to define the functionality of swiping action, while on Android, it is swiping up and down. The good news is that these settings are opaque to the developer as long as standard practices are followed and only come into play when dealing with custom gestures.

Even if we just consider mobile web, different browsers on the same operating systems will work differently with assistive technologies. This is also true of websites outside of mobile. Even if the author follows guidelines to make their site work on a given screen reader, there is no guarantee that other combinations of browsers and screen readers will respect those specifications. In short, the accessibility APIs are not interoperable, which makes both writing applications, and testing them a tedious task for teams, and a painful experience for users.

---

[2] https://developer.android.com/guide/topics/ui/accessibility
[3] https://developer.apple.com/design/human-interface-guidelines/accessibility/overview/introduction/

Other sources of fragmentation, and hence accounting for potentially different user experiences come from

- Memory on the phone model

- Battery life

- Network availability and speed

- Data usage

Fragmentation is also a great reason to invest in design and development upfront, rather than coming back and having to verify fixes on the various combinations of devices and configurations.

Smaller Screen Sizes and Conflicting Guidelines

For reference, the range of viewport widths on the market starts at 320 pixels (iPhone 5) to over 1000 pixels[4] for some tablets.

We might run into conflicting guidelines because of limited screen real estate on touchscreen devices. For example, having large tap targets so users with motor impairments or partial vision can reliably activate components is considered good practice. Another guideline is to avoid two-way scrolling (horizontal and vertical) for blind users. Firstly, the visual presentation of content is irrelevant to blind users. Secondly, having content spaced out, or out of the viewport makes it more tedious, and sometimes impossible to navigate.

Customizing UI components to scale in one direction upon increasing magnification is one way to address this conflict. For elements such as tables and carousels, it is trickier and is often addressed by either

1. Abbreviating content in tables to allow more columns

2. Allowing users to switch to landscape mode for more room brings us to our next mobile-specific point

Wearables take these challenges to a whole new level, with viewports as small as 1.5-1.7 inches.

---

[4]https://mediag.com/blog/popular-screen-resolutions-designing-for-all/

Orientation

Supporting both portrait and landscape orientations not only helps with horizontally scrolling components, but also helps people with motor impairments, who might have their phone mounted on a wheelchair or desk, and so use the device in the orientation most convenient for them. Persisting the orientation setting between sessions, and maintaining the user's position on a page when switching orientation in the middle of a session is the best experience.

On Android applications, orientation change can trigger a page reload if the page's lifecycle events are not handled to support a smooth transition. It will require overriding the methods related to saved instances of an Activity,[5] and should be paid special attention to in cases of forms and scrollable content.

Release Cycles and Long-Tail Adoption

Another great reason for upfront investment in inclusive design and development also comes from how mobile applications are released. Unlike websites that can be updated immediately, mobile applications go through application stores (Play Store for Android, and App Store for iOS) and can take a few hours to several days for approval and distribution to users.

The next step is for users to download a new version unless they have opted for auto-updates. This means it will take a long time (sometimes years) before an app version with severe bugs is completely out of use. Integrating accessibility, robust testing practices, and CI integration for mobile is much better than retroactively fixing issues.

Haptics and Other Sensors

Website design relies on visual and auditory feedback methods to convey information. User experience designers on mobile also need to factor in haptic (vibration) feedback. We are all familiar with text messages/call notifications with vibration. While vibration is an additional way to get most users' attention, it is the only way for a deaf user who is not looking at their phone to know they are getting a call. It is also an excellent method to enrich notifications of critical information such as input errors.

---

[5] https://developer.android.com/guide/topics/resources/runtime-changes

Note that using haptics can cause sensory overload, especially for users with cognitive impairments, or nuisance for people with tremors. Users should have the option to fine-tune their notification preferences, including the ability to turn off haptic feedback.

Data Usage

As we discussed earlier, data plans, network availability, and hardware limitations add several layers of complexity to the already fragmented mobile ecosystem. Efficient use of network resources reduces latency and lag on higher-end devices in addition to making a usable experience for lower-end ones. When building an app with data usage in mind, it's worth asking the following questions:

1.   Do the designs account for network error states?

2.   Does it make sense to use local device storage in case of network unavailability?

Two-Way Scrolling

We have all seen carousels of images or cards on an otherwise vertically scrollable page. For people with mobility impairments, performing gestures on a touchscreen device can result in unintended behavior. For people who use magnification or larger text sizes, reading through content in both directions is even more cumbersome. These effects are compounded by having limited screen real estate on mobile devices, as you can see in Figure 5-1.

Figure 5-1. *Mobile screen with horizontally and vertically scrolling content*

We will now walk-through a few case studies on applications of mobile-first features and how they can make our physical and digital experiences more accessible.

Case Study: Indoor and Outdoor Wayfinding

Aiding wayfinding or navigation in the physical world is one of the most fascinating areas of accessibility. Smartphones make navigation easier than ever, with turn-by-turn instructions, street view, and a host of other tools at our fingertips. Almost all users with disabilities face challenges getting from point A to point B safely and efficiently. As an example, we will go through some challenges of pedestrian navigation and how smartphones can help address them.

Screen readers can dictate turn-by-turn instructions to a blind user. That takes care of the efficiency part of the problem. For doing so safely by avoiding obstacles and traffic, the user needs more information about their surroundings.

During COVID-19, maintaining the six-feet separation recommended by the CDC was particularly difficult for visually impaired people.[6] Not only did it put others at health risk, but also made them susceptible to potentially offending others who did not realize that these people couldn't see.

The same principle applies when the user is on a busy street or open space. Smartphone cameras and on-device machine learning for image recognition make the recognition and notification about surrounding objects possible even with no network connectivity. These notifications can be in the form of voice commands, haptic feedback (vibration), or a combination of the two. Devices such as the iPhone now also come with LIDAR (Light Detection and Ranging) sensors that aid in accurately alerting the user to oncoming traffic and obstacles.

One thing to note is that these powerful cameras and sensors are only available on higher-end phones at the time of writing this, which might be financially inaccessible for many.

Case Study: Floating Action Buttons

Floating action buttons (FABs) were introduced as part of Google's material design guidelines. Figure 5-2 is a screenshot depicting a floating action button.

---

[6] https://iovs.arvojournals.org/article.aspx?articleid=2775975

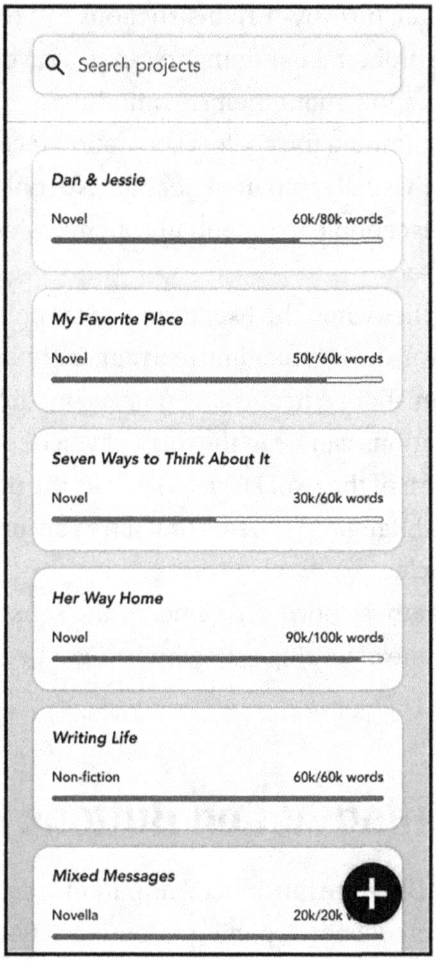

Figure 5-2. *Mobile screen with a floating action button*

FABs are used to provide an easily reachable item (being on the bottom right, closest to the right thumb), which triggers the primary action on a screen. For sighted users, a FAB takes the most prominent place on the screen since it is highest on the z-axis according to material design guidelines.

A screen reader user, who is swiping or tabbing through elements, will reach the FAB last, and in some cases never, for instance in infinite streams. For partially sighted users, it might present another challenge since it covers part of the content. This is less of a problem because in most cases, it is possible to scroll to see the hidden content. There are two ways to address this for screen reader users, as shown in Figure 5-3:

1. Change the focus order so the user first focuses on the FAB and then through other elements at the top of the screen

2. Move the FAB action to the top of the screen if the user is using a screen reader

   i. Be visually consistent with the focus order

   ii. Avoid hiding content under the FAB

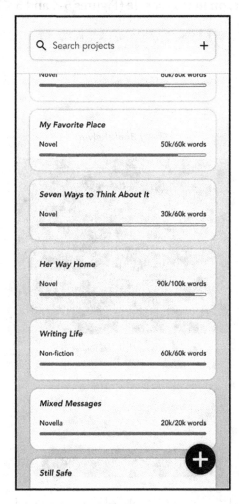

Figure 5-3. *Mobile screen with a floating action button, and the same action in the toolbar*

Case Study: Ephemeral Experiences

Instagram has over 500 million monthly story users, and a third of the most-viewed stories come from businesses.[7] Snapchat has over 400 million monthly users.[8] While ephemeral experiences provide a great way for people to engage with each other, and with businesses, they bring a host of accessibility challenges.

Let's take an example of the following series of pictures and videos as part of a story posted by a furniture store, on items for sale (Figures 5-4 and 5-5).

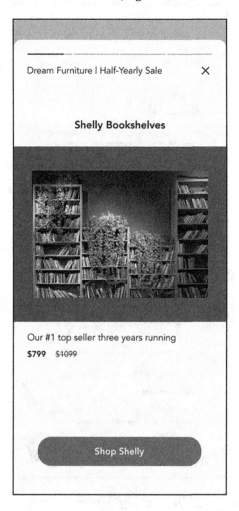

Figure 5-4. *Mobile screen with a story-format ephemeral content. The current focus is the first image out of four items*

---

[7]https://business.instagram.com/
[8]www.statista.com/statistics/626835/number-of-monthly-active-snapchat-users/

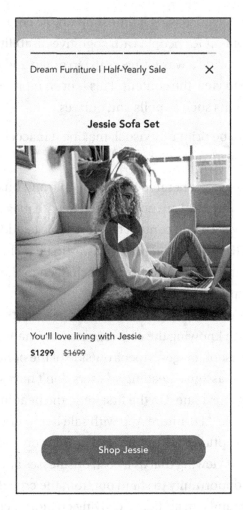

Figure 5-5. *Mobile screen with a story-format ephemeral content with four items. The current focus is the last item, a video*

On the surface, these stories are just a collection of images, text, and videos – UI components that we discussed in Chapter 3. Now, let's ask ourselves what makes ephemeral content in this format different from these standard UI components, and which part of the experience needs attention.

    a.   Each story item is visible only for a few seconds, making it challenging for people with cognitive disabilities to consume content

Once a story is being viewed, having a time limit on the content makes it difficult or impossible to digest content for people with cognitive disabilities such as anxiety or ADHD.[9] Most platforms provide a way for users to tap or tap and hold so users can pause and have additional time to view the content. This is even more important if the content includes interactive elements such as polls and quizzes.

    b.   Content tends to be primarily visual, making it inaccessible for users with complete or partial vision loss

Most of this content is user-generated, that is, people and businesses upload their own content to platforms and are not required to add image labels or captions/audio descriptions to videos. Giving content creators tools to add alternative text for images and videos at the time of upload is a great way to be inclusive. Another option is using image recognition and ASR (Automatic Speech Recognition) to assign labels for unlabeled images, and captions for videos.

For stories with multiple items, such as the one above, another dimension of complexity for the user is in knowing the context, and how many items there are, similar to what we would do in a list of images/videos outside of the ephemeral format. For stories with multiple items, assign a heading so users don't have to go through all items in a story to proceed to the next one. On the first item, the heading should have all the relevant details. For example, "Furniture App with sale items story," "4 images, 1 video."

Adding image labels, captions, and audio descriptions do add a few steps to the creation process. Instead of viewing that as a cost, businesses and creators can reap outsized returns and the opportunity to stand out from the crowd, and strengthen their reputations as inclusive brands. In addition to giving creators a chance to connect with millions of underserved users with disabilities they wouldn't otherwise reach, these measures bring several other benefits. In a recent study, 70% of Gen-Z participants said they trust brands that are more inclusive, which directly translates into buying habits.[10] As discussed in Chapter 3, labels and captions also help with SEO (Search Engine Optimization). Many of these benefits are quantifiable, even in the short term. Platforms can encourage creators to adopt inclusive content practices by making this data widely available.

---

[9] www.cdc.gov/ncbddd/adhd/facts.html

[10] https://advertiseonbing-blob.azureedge.net/blob/bingads/media/insight/whitepapers/2020/07-july/inclusive-marketing/microsoft-advertising-whitepaper-the-psychology-of-inclusion-and-the-effects-in-advertising-gen-z-final.pdf?s_cid=en-us-gct-web-src_contributor-sub_oth-cam_hubspot

Similar to viewer considerations, having creator tools with appropriate labels, groupings, and heading structures for screen reader and keyboard access ensures that people with vision loss/motor impairments can engage with their audience, and perform their jobs independently (e.g., marketers).

    c.   Custom gestures such as press and hold or swiping can be difficult for users with motor impairments

Tapping on videos can unintentionally turn sound on, for example. For users who might be using eye-tracking devices, keyboards, or mounted displays, it is important to make sure that these interactions are keyboard accessible.

Implementation

These stories are, in the end, just a list of images, text boxes, form elements, and videos presented in a new format. The technical implementation of assigning labels, adding captions, or adding heading structures to match the hierarchy of elements will look exactly like it would if these elements were in a nonephemeral format.

The development team can also take the experience one step further by providing custom settings in the application to offer a list-based version of stories, with

- Buttons for links to learn more/buy

- Standard input components such as text box for quizzes and polls

- The chosen font size for captions

The content will still be ephemeral in that it will expire in 24 hours, or another timeframe, but in this view, the user can scroll or tab through it at their own pace, with their choice of assistive technology, without special gestures. Figures 5-6 and 5-7 show examples of what this might look like for the furniture app sale story.

Figure 5-6. *Mobile screen with the same content from the story presented as cards*

Figure 5-7. *Mobile screen with the same content from the story presented as cards*

Summary

- The WCAG 2.0 standards that form the basis of most regulations were released in 2008. Mobile mapping for WCAG 2.0 was last published in 2015, for a set of guidelines written five years before that. Since then we have seen at least seven new releases each of the Android and iOS operating systems.

- The rapidly evolving mobile space has outpaced the documentation and adoption of these guidelines but in the meantime platform-specific documentation for the

- Android and iOS accessibility provide a framework, though it is no replacement for talking to your users and understanding their needs.

- Between iOS and Android, there are different accessibility settings that introduce an added layer of complexity to the already fragmented mobile ecosystem. Fragmentation is also a great reason to invest in design and development upfront, rather than coming back and having to verify fixes on the various combinations of devices and configurations.

- Another reason for upfront investment in inclusive design and development also comes from how mobile applications are released. It will take a long time (sometimes years) before an app version with severe bugs is completely out of use. Integrating accessibility, robust testing practices, and CI integration for mobile is much better than retroactively fixing issues.

CHAPTER 6

We Built It, Now What?

When we discussed testing and quality assurance in the previous chapter, it meant checking for issues before the product goes out to customers. One way to do this is manually, where real people go through an application and report issues they come across. Another way is through automated tests that run at certain times during the code writing and building processes. In this chapter, we'll review how manual and automated testing close the loop on sustainable accessible design.

Automated Testing

Automated testing means programmatically running parts of an application to make sure they work as expected under different scenarios, and to prevent errors (regressions) if the underlying code changes at a later date.

For example, we're checking that text on a button (Figure 6-1) has sufficient color contrast with its background so it is easier for users with visual impairments such as color blindness to read the text.

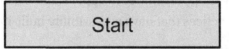

Figure 6-1. *Figure of a start button with a light blue background and black text*

At a later date, the design changes to have a darker background color (Figure 6-2), which fails the contrast check.

Figure 6-2. *Figure of a start button with a dark blue background and black text*

© Sukriti Chadha 2023
S. Chadha, *Beyond Accessibility Compliance*, https://doi.org/10.1007/978-1-4842-7948-9_6

This test will fail as soon as the developer makes the change locally (on their own machine), or in the pull request phase (when their changes are compared to the latest version of the main application). The feedback loop in the absence of this test would have been much longer (manual tester or user ➤ feedback channel ➤ project manager ➤ engineering team ➤ tester), where the problem would go unfixed until a user complains, or there was a manual audit.

Advantages of automated testing:

1. Automated tests are especially effective when application development is decentralized, that is, several different teams are making changes to the same codebase.

2. If different versions of the application are available due to experimentation, automated testing can cover different combinations of the holistic experience, all of which would be time-consuming if done manually.

3. While it is clear that some level of manual oversight is necessary, automated testing helps surface low-hanging fruit to free up time for more complicated error discovery. It can also be integrated with the continuous delivery process. By highlighting the error in a developer's workflow, the feedback loop is much shorter than manual testing practices.

4. In large distributed teams, automated testing results can also help identify teams that might need more education or accessibility training, as well as opportunities to apply standard design components/practices that have accessibility built-in.

Limitations of automated testing

1. Currently, the subset of WCAG guidelines automated tests can check for is limited to a handful, especially on mobile. These include labels, color contrast, punctuations, clickable span focus, and others listed later in this section. Of course, it is possible for developers to write their own automated tests to cover other guidelines. This is time-consuming, although often worth it in the long run.

2. These checks cannot verify the semantic accuracy of accessible content. For example, a label check can ensure that a label is present, but it cannot check whether the label is a good one or an accurate one.

3. If the views to be checked are not already covered by tests, it might require some initial investment into adding test coverage.

4. Test reports are only effective if they are followed up on. Disabling or deleting a test are two quick ways to get a pull request merged if it fails an accessibility check.

Automated test frameworks for mobile are available as open source libraries, for example, GTXiLib (iOS)[1] and ATF (Accessibility Test Framework for Android).[2] There are other free and paid tools that offer bespoke functionality for automated checks. Currently, open source checks on Android and iOS allow for the following checks:

ATF

1. Speakable Text Present

2. Redundant Description

3. Touch Target Size

4. Text Contrast

5. Editable Content Description

6. Duplicate Speakable Text

7. Clickable Span

8. Duplicate Clickable Bounds

9. Image Contrast Check

10. Class Name Check

11. Traversal Order Check

GTXiLib

---

[1] https://github.com/google/GTXiLib

[2] https://developer.android.com/codelabs/a11y-testing-espresso

The GTXiLib Toolkit integrates with existing test frameworks and can run accessibility checks on all child elements from the given root. This means that accessibility or platform teams can enable these checks for developers who write integration tests with relatively no extra effort on their part. Currently, GTXiLib can check for:

1. Link Purpose Unclear Check

2. Accessibility Label Present

3. Accessibility Label-Trait Overlap

4. Accessibility Label Not Punctuated

5. Accessibility Traits: Element fails if it has conflicting accessibility traits

6. Touch target size

7. Contrast ratio (Label)

8. Option for custom checks

Scanners

Halfway between automated and manual testing are scanners, which scan each screen you manually visit and find accessibility violations. Examples of these are the Android Accessibility Scanner, and the XCode inspector on iOS. On the web, tools such as Lighthouse scan websites for a subset of accessibility errors.

The Accessibility Scanner on Android is a free application downloaded from the Google Play Store,[3] which can analyze a screen or a series of screens, and generate shareable reports. Figure 6-3 is an example of a scan from a food delivery app, followed by a report (Figure 6-4).

---

[3] https://play.google.com/store/apps/details?id=com.google.android.apps.accessibility.auditor

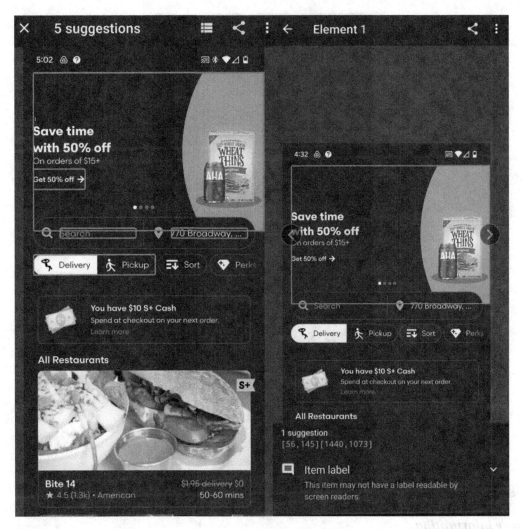

Figure 6-3. *Two screenshots from an accessibility scan of a food delivery app. The first one shows all detected issues highlighted with an orange outline. The second one is a selected issue, which brings up details of the element's accessibility issue. In this case, it is a missing label*

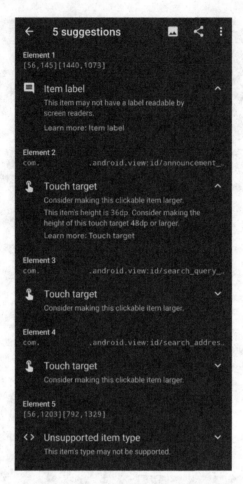

Figure 6-4. *Screenshot of a shareable report generated by the Android Accessibility Scanner that details accessibility issues found on the screen, remedies, and links to more information*

On iOS, the XCode inspector is part of the development environment that analyses screens on the simulator (virtual device). Scanners are particularly useful for teams that do not have automated testing practices in place. By highlighting basic errors, scanners can save a lot of time in the manual testing phase and leave time for checks including semantic verification.

Manual Testing

The most comprehensive checklist for accessibility compliance is the one published by the W3C WAI (Web Accessibility Initiative), which can be found at `www.w3.org/WAI/WCAG21/quickref/`.

The list contains over 70 items, and can at first be overwhelming. Only a subset of these items applies to any given product. If usability (not just compliance) is the goal, checklists can provide a great jumping-off point, but much like the tiered approach to prioritizing audit reports discussed in Chapter 3, teams will need to weave accessibility testing with their manual testing routine including bug bashes (where members of a product team dedicate a specific amount of time together to test their features and to discover software regressions), sign-off processes, and occasional audits.

An effective manual test strategy will answer the following questions:

- Which are the most important user flows?

- What is already tested in the automated process?

- How often do we manually test our application?

  - Regular testing (daily, weekly)

  - Release testing

  - Bug bash sessions

  - Audits

- What should be tested at each of these stages?

The preceding processes are in decreasing order of frequency of testing. Core user flows must be tested against all applicable criteria with as many of these steps as possible, followed by secondary and less critical user flows.

One practice that has worked extremely well in my experience was creating user personas and picking at least one per bug bash, and taking turns using the feature we were testing with related assistive technology. Bug bashing sessions are particularly powerful because they are typically done with the entire development team including designers, engineers, and product managers. Firstly, it helps the team learn how people with disabilities use the product and empathize with them. Secondly, it uncovers opportunities and not just bugs in the application. Following is a list of sample personas for a job application site:

Persona 1

A blind Talkback or VoiceOver writer who is looking for a copywriting role

Persona 2

Engineering manager with a hearing impairment hiring for software developers

Persona 3

Partially sighted keyboard user with a motor impairment looking for a store manager position

Persona 4

College student with short-term memory looking for art internships and career advice

---

Tip   One neat trick in manually testing a mobile application is to test with an external keyboard because, in the process, it checks for criteria including labels, focus order, the grouping of elements, hierarchy, links, and focus traps.

Evaluating Third-Party Testing Vendors

Sometimes teams may choose to hire external consultants or vendors for automated or manual testing support. You are basically trying to answer two questions here:

- Is it more feasible to build the infrastructure in-house?

- If not, which vendor do we pick?

The following evaluation criteria will help benchmark internal solutions with these service providers in the test run:

1. Latency

For CI integration, you want the checks to run in parallel with the regular test suite for a short feedback loop and PR merge times. This also factors in the turnaround time of the generated report. For manual audits, this is less of a concern.

2. Accuracy

Pick 2-3 user flows that span across multiple screens and make a list of known issues (you can hire a consultant to do this as well). In the evaluation, make sure all known issues are highlighted, to avoid false positives (or false negatives).

3. Scalability

Make sure the system can scale to handle simultaneous builds and large test suites, especially in teams with hundreds of developers working on the same repository.

4. Price (integration cost)

How much upfront effort (time and resources) is it going to take for the team to integrate and maintain third-party software with existing build systems? How does this compare with building that same infrastructure on top of open source frameworks?

5. Licencing and vendor fee

Manual testing: Is it more feasible to hire accessibility testing experts in-house?

The benefit of doing this is that internal testers will become dedicated product experts over time and build relationships with development teams. The downside is individual testers take time to ramp up, and may not scale with fluctuating needs. If the demand for manual testing varies over time, it might make more economic sense to hire a third-party vendor with that flexibility. A hybrid model with a few in-house testers and additional testers when needed could be the best option for some companies.

Third-party vendors tend to have varying pricing models. They can charge in a number of different ways:

- a lump sum

- per hour

- per run

- per screen

- per issue found

- per build

- per developer

For example, if a vendor's pricing model is based on the number of developers working on a repository, you would only want to count the developers who work on user-facing features that impact accessibility.

6. Coverage

    a. How much of the application is covered?

     b.   Of all the criteria you want to be tested, how many are
          covered? You can use WCAG guidelines as a baseline for this
          calculation, but a better baseline would be only guidelines
          that apply to your product. You could write your own using
          WCAG as a framework to get the best of both.

7. SLAs

Does the vendor have a reasonable service level agreement, that is, how much time they will take to address issues once reported? How will the reporting work, and is it in line with current workflows? For example, if there is a known issue with their system, will the team be notified? If the team notices an issue, is there an easy way for them to get in touch with the vendor's team? The level of support needs to be good enough to justify not building a testing team internally.

8. Actionability of reports

Any reports generated by the third party, either manually or automatically, should have screenshots, detailed explanations of errors, WCAG, or other guidelines the issue pertains to, as well as suggested solutions including code samples.

One metric that would be incredibly useful in these reports, that no vendor in my experience currently displays, is the number of users (globally or in specific countries) that live with the relevant disability and would be affected by the issue.

9. Parseability of reports

The ability to filter and sort issues by type, screen, severity, and other parameters is key to making the reports easily digestible and hence actionable for whoever is responsible for triaging and assignment. A thorough report loses a lot of its power if it takes a lot to feed it into your workflow.

10. Customizability

Related to actionability is how customizable the reports and the workflows surrounding them are. Is it possible to extract information from the reports into an API that powers internal workflows and dashboards? If not, can the reports be exported into Excel or other document formats for further analysis and assignment?

Note   API stands for Application Programming Interface, which means a way for systems or computers to share information using a set of predetermined rules. In this case, it could mean an internal reporting application requests specific information from the report to display and notify teams in their preferred format.

Customer Service: How to Help Customers and Escalate Critical Issues

If you have an inclusive, comprehensive product development strategy and testing practices discussed before, doing this part becomes much easier because ideally, very few people will need to contact support.

Guidelines and best practices help avoid known issues. However, each user has their own unique way of engaging with products. In the accessibility context, there might be unforeseen interactions, and opportunities for improvement that only users with certain limitations, use cases, or intersection of disabilities will understand.

The motivation is no different than support pages, FAQs,[4] and feedback channels for all users. Making sure users with disabilities are able to reach relevant teams with requests and feedback through accessible channels is important to ensure they don't get stuck or feel unheard. For example, if phone is the only support channel offered, it might make sense to evaluate email or chat alternatives for people with hearing impairments or communication anxiety.

The second step in the process is to train agents and customer experience teams in identifying accessibility issues, determining their criticality, and escalating them to the right teams. It also involves using inclusive language in their responses, as well as help pages or FAQ documentation. A customer service guide published by the Ontario Education Service Corporation[5] covers basic principles as well as inclusive language guidelines for specific disabilities. The ADA website also has a document with quick tips.[6]

---

[4] Frequently Asked Questions
[5] www.sgdsb.on.ca/upload/documents/accessibility-tips-booklet_eng.pdf
[6] https://adata.org/factsheet/quicktips-customer-service

Reports and suggestions from real users will also serve as a data source for measuring the success of a team's accessibility efforts. This data source is reliable only when the product team has an effective relationship with users, and they feel invested enough to share feedback.

Similar to holistic audits, these channels can also highlight systemic issues in big distributed teams that can be either centrally resolved or combined into support documentation. A few metrics to track success on this side of the equation are

- Number of issues reported relative to application size

- Percentage of issues resolved

- Average time to resolve issues

- Average and total agent time spent on resolution

- Customer satisfaction ratings

Summary

- Automated testing means programmatically running parts of an application to make sure they work as expected under different scenarios, and to prevent errors (regressions) if the underlying code changes at a later date.

- Advantages of automated testing include shorter feedback cycles between discovery and remediation of bugs and identification of systemic issues in large distributed teams, thereby freeing teams to focus on innovation.

- Halfway between automated and manual testing are scanners, which scan each screen you manually visit and find accessibility violations. This is useful for teams that do not have automated testing practices in place. By highlighting basic errors, scanners can save time in the manual testing phase and leave time for checks including semantic verification.

- The most comprehensive checklist for accessibility compliance is the one published by the W3C WAI (Web Accessibility Initiative), which can be found at www.w3.org/WAI/WCAG21/quickref/.

- One practice that works extremely well in the absence of direct user feedback is creating *user personas* and taking turns using features with related assistive technology as those users.

- In-house testing experts become dedicated product experts over time and build relationships with development teams. The downside is individual testers take time to ramp up, and may not scale with fluctuating needs. If the demand for manual testing varies over time, it might make more economic sense to hire a third-party vendor with that flexibility.

- Making sure users with disabilities are able to reach relevant teams with requests and feedback through accessible channels is important to ensure they don't get stuck or feel unheard.

CHAPTER 7

The Next Frontier – Expanding the Definition of Accessibility

Before we dive into the specifics, let's imagine a few days in the lives of people with disabilities using current and emerging technologies 20 years from now.

A Day in the Life: 2040

Jane

Jane is a freelance journalist in New York City. Jane grew up in Italy, and is fluent in English but speaks with a heavy accent. She has cataracts in both eyes that limit 80% of her vision. Jane enjoys walking in Central Park, visiting museums, and exploring new restaurants with friends.

7:00 am

Alexa wakes up Jane by playing her favorite song, and turning on her espresso machine.

8:00 am

Jane opens the refrigerator, which tells her she has a week left on those eggs from Whole Foods, and two days on the milk. More will be delivered tomorrow. Jane makes her breakfast and leaves for a client meeting in her self-driving car.

8:50 am

The car is now stuck in traffic and Jane is running late. She decides to walk the last two blocks to get there faster. The car drops Jane off and leaves to make her some extra money as an Uber in the meantime. Jane is now guided with turn-by-turn instructions, and information on her surroundings, as well as traffic on her way to the meeting.

© Sukriti Chadha 2023
S. Chadha, *Beyond Accessibility Compliance*, https://doi.org/10.1007/978-1-4842-7948-9_7

Her smart AR glasses recognize the client she is meeting, highlighting a path from her to the table. As she is walking toward their table, her watch signals her to stop with haptic feedback, because the glasses have recognized freshly mopped floors, which she walks around.

12:00 pm

Jane's car picks her up for lunch with a friend at the MoMA (Museum of Modern Art). She walks around the museum with her audio tour guide and asks questions about the pieces she comes across. At the lunch table, her glasses enlarge the physical menu. On her watch, she can also get the braille representation for items she points at. She can hear the entire menu, navigate by gestures over the physical menu through headings, or choose to only listen to items recommended/highlighted for her.

2:00 pm

Before leaving the museum, Jane stops by the museum store to explore. She walks around the store while her glasses scan items she is looking at, and generate descriptions of items, their price, whether they are on sale, and comparisons with similar items at other stores. Her sighted friend is intrigued by how efficiently Jane is able to shop and asks to use Jane's glasses. They both decide to buy a tea kettle, the friend pays with a credit card, and Jane pays with her watch. Jane heads home to wrap up her remaining work for the day.

5:00 pm

Jane walks in Central Park with just her smart glasses and watch, which she turns to haptic-only mode. This allows her to get vibration feedback about the severity and direction of potential obstacles, and enjoy uninterrupted music from Vandaveer, a folksy bluegrass-but-not-bluegrass Kentucky-based band that Spotify put on her Discover Weekly playlist. In case you are wondering why this was here, I work for Spotify, hehe:)

6:30 pm

Jane asks her voice assistant to order dinner for her and her roommate from her favorite place in Italian (yes, she ordered Italian food in Italian). The assistant makes the call in English and places the order while Jane picks a show to watch. She watches a couple of episodes with the roommate. They each have their headphones, Jane's are set up to receive audio descriptions, while the roommate's are not.

Joe

Joe is a 65-year-old retired Air Force veteran who lives with his wife Jamie in Chattanooga, Tennessee. He likes to read the news, go on walks with Jamie, and spend a few hours a week on his flight simulator. He was recently diagnosed with Parkinson's, which can affect motor control, and speech and cause tremors.

9:00 am

Joe and Jamie go to the local coffee shop and read the news on their phones. Joe selects and reads items with eye and head tracking technology built into his phone instead of tapping with his fingers, while Jamie, who is running out of charge switches her news app to dark mode. They return home and spend the afternoon watching birds and squirrels from their back porch.

1:00 pm

Joe and Jamie facetime with their grandchildren from their tablet while eating lunch. The grandchildren turn on captions. Joe gets a reminder about taking his weight, vitals, and assessment on his phone before a follow-up appointment with his physician over video. During this time, his voice assistant is training the AI model in the background to help recognize Joe's speech as his disease progresses.

6:00 pm

It's time for Joe to switch on his flight simulator and connect with his virtual co-pilot and friend. Joe has a setup with adaptive controls, and eye-tracking software to land an A320 at Telluride, one of the world's most dangerous airports. Jamie reads in the next room, assured that Joe's watch which tracks his vitals will communicate with the home assistant in case she needs to step in. Same for Joe.

8:00 pm

Joe enters a lottery for a ticket on the space flight next Veteran's Day. On the form, he is asked about his medical history, which will be used to determine his training and additional considerations for the team.

Jay

Jay is a high school student in Haryana, India who wants to study computer science in college. He will be the first in his family to attend college. Jay has ADHD and recently temporarily lost hearing due to an ear infection. His school holds half the lessons online and half in person. In his free time, Jay enjoys watching and playing soccer with friends and working on programming projects.

8:00 am

Jay joins his online class where the teacher goes over recursion, and the class is asked to complete a live programming exercise. The video conferencing tool they use has live captions, and an option to ask questions in chat, or by raising your hand to ask verbally. While the interactivity and options to engage are great, they can be overwhelming and sometimes distracting. The application lets Jay only see the captions and slides instead of everything (instructor, everyone in the class, and the stream of questions and comments in chat). He can also use this setting outdoors when his phone service is unreliable. At the end of the lecture, he receives an email with the transcript and edits it to highlight the portions to review instead of taking notes.

1:00 pm

Classes end with a lunch break in between. Jay recaps learnings from the day, takes a nap in the afternoon, and works on a group project with his classmates.

5:00 pm

Jay walks to the neighborhood park to play soccer. On his way, he is biking in front of a car that wants to pass him. He gets a haptic notification on his watch indicating he needs to pay attention behind him. He veers to the side of the road to let the car pass. At half-time when the team is deciding on a strategy, he uses the live transcribe app on his phone and responds verbally.

6:30 pm

Jay and his family watch Parasite, the Korean thriller, with subtitles of course. His grandmother, who has limited hearing and never learned to read, uses a real-time sign language app to help her follow the story.

Although the days portrayed above are hypothetical, they are not far from millions of people's real-life experiences. Some of the solutions might seem futuristic but many of them either already exist, or have versions under development. Assistive technology has long paved the way for mainstream technology. The examples above are just a subset of how assistive technology, powered by computer vision, AI-powered personalization, image processing, XR (Augmented, Virtual and Mixed Reality), IoT (Internet of Things), and smartphones will come together to create frictionless experiences that enrich *everyone's* lives.

Microsoft released Seeing AI, which allows blind users to use their camera and hear their phone describe objects it sees around them. It can also help read documents, scan barcodes, and recognize faces among other applications.[1] iPhone models starting from 2020 are also equipped with LIDAR[2] (distance sensing), which, among other applications, can significantly increase depth perception and the ability to navigate around obstacles.

---

[1] www.microsoft.com/en-us/garage/wall-of-fame/seeing-ai/
[2] https://oceanservice.noaa.gov/facts/lidar.html

Performance, Localization, and Financial Accessibility

In Chapter 2, we discussed functional user needs based on the type of disability. Now let's talk about other aspects of inclusion that are less obvious, and that also happen to be great business levers.

Technical Performance

By performance, we mean an application's speed and efficiency, which has a direct impact on all top-line metrics including acquisition, engagement, and retention. For example, Amazon and Walmart saw a 1% increase in sales every 100 milliseconds of startup time.[3] Similarly, Google reported that a half a second increase in waiting time results in a 20% decrease in traffic[4]

Performance metrics you could monitor include:

- Cold start time, meaning the time it takes between opening an application, and for the content to be available/visible

- Data usage

- Application size – memory usage for installing the application

- Memory usage (app size and storage) – once the application is running, the amount of memory it requires to store data on the device

- Battery consumption

Performance also relates to another aspect of digital inclusion that is seldom discussed – financial inclusion. Mobile devices are more economically feasible than laptops and desktop computers, apart from supporting the most versatile use cases (not restricted to a location). But even within the mobile space, the performance

---

[3] www.globaldots.com/resources/blog/how-website-speed-affects-conversion-rates/
[4] https://ieeexplore.ieee.org/document/7280867

characteristics mentioned above are vastly different from an entry-level price point to the highest-end device. As of 2022, phones are available for as low as $20,[5] while iPhones begin at $429.[6]

As a rule of thumb, if your application or mobile website is functional and performant on lower-end devices, it will work even better on the higher-end ones. Optimizing for the lowest common denominator, also known as progressive enhancement, is a win-win. This is not to say that teams should feel limited in using additional resources that come with higher-end devices to create more delightful experiences. On mobile, modularization by paradigms such as Instant apps[7] and App Bundles[8] encourage breaking down products into individually functioning pieces to tackle some of these challenges. Apps such as Facebook Messenger, Spotify, and Twitter even have a lite version of their regular apps to reach a broader audience with lower-end devices. Some companies use smaller native apps, and others use web-based Progressive Web Apps[9] (PWAs). Starbucks is a great example of a PWA, that is, **99.84% smaller** than Starbucks' existing iOS app, making the web app a favorite among its users. As a result, they doubled the number of web users who place orders each day, with desktop users now ordering at about the same rate as mobile users.[10]

Localization

At least for consumer products, reaching as broad a customer base as possible is an evergreen goal. Accessibility is one way to achieve it. Localization or offering the product in more than one language is another effective way.

We previously discussed how thinking about design with various languages helps with dynamic sizing and relative placement of UI components. However, we can no longer think of localization as only applicable to text-based content.

---

[5] www.techradar.com/news/the-land-of-the-20-smartphone

[6] www.apple.com/shop/buy-iphone/iphone-se

[7] https://developer.android.com/topic/google-play-instant

[8] https://developer.android.com/guide/app-bundle

[9] https://developer.mozilla.org/en-US/docs/Web/Progressive_web_apps/Introduction

[10] www.simicart.com/blog/progressive-web-apps-examples/

As voice interaction is becoming mainstream, it is important to look at not just how a user understands the content they see, but also how *they* are understood. This includes factoring in different languages as well as accents. Speech detection is an extremely complex domain that needs large datasets and complex algorithms to work well, which brings us to the next point.

Multimodal Input and Output

Voice assistants add another option to interact with devices that have traditionally been primarily visual. Not only is this a great resource for visually impaired users, but also for those who can't read, or prefer not to. (Personally, I mostly use voice typing instead of typing on my phone.)

At the same time, it has limited use for people with hearing and speech impairments. These can be traditionally defined as disabilities, or limitations introduced by context (being in a noisy environment), accents, or uncommon speech patterns.

To call an experience truly inclusive, the best bet is to have multiple modes of engagement (visual, auditory, and haptic) so the user has the ability to pick what suits them best at a given moment.

Interoperability and the Role of Platforms

While it is the responsibility of individual products to be ultimately responsible for their inclusion practices, and the subsequent business outcomes, the more integrated these practices become through IDEs and platform development tools, the easier it is for teams to do the right thing as part of their everyday workflow. It also sets standard expectations for users who interact with multiple products every day.

Another dimension of interoperability comes from assistive technologies working predictably with different combinations of browsers, mobile operating systems, and devices. This will be impossible until accessibility becomes part of mainstream tech conferences, open source projects, hackathons, and the overall conversation around technology.

Mindset

Accessibility has largely been focused on making information and media consumable for people with disabilities. Technology has enabled millions of people to work from home, monetize their creative passions, and engage with the digital world in unprecedented ways. We can no longer afford to think of inclusion as a one-way street where most people are just consumers of content. Inclusive tools that allow people with disabilities to partake in a creator-driven, remote-first economy will have a huge advantage over their counterparts.

In the same vein, businesses that embrace a remote or hybrid office model not only have the flexibility to hire geographically diverse candidates, but also people who would otherwise not be able to travel to work every day. According to Accenture research, the US GDP could get as much as a $25 billion boost if even an additional 1% of Americans with disabilities were able to participate in the labor force.[11] There is currently an over 40% difference in the employment rates between people with disabilities and others.[12] The advantage of recruiting from this diverse pool of untapped talent comes with the responsibility of rethinking employee resources, work-related tools, support, and hiring practices.

Nobody is exempt from thinking about disability inclusion. At some point in our lives, it's highly likely that we will either face a temporary or situational disability or be a caretaker for someone else. In Chapter 3, where we discussed basic principles of accessibility (as well as earlier in this chapter), where we went over emerging trends, one pattern is clear – We can treat assistive technology as either a checkbox item, or we can treat it as inspiration for the next generation of cutting-edge technology. The determining factors are a team's long-term focus, imagination, and ability to build world-class products.

---

[11] www.accenture.com/_acnmedia/pdf-89/accenture-disability-inclusion-research-report.pdf

[12] www.brookings.edu/blog/the-avenue/2018/07/25/only-four-out-of-ten-working-age-adults-with-disabilities-are-employed/

Summary

- Another aspect of digital inclusion that is seldom discussed is financial inclusion. Optimizing for less expensive devices also means it will work even better on the higher-end ones.

- Localization, or offering the product in more than one language, is another effective way to reach as broad an audience as possible. This includes factoring in different languages as well as accents.

- To call an experience truly inclusive, the best bet is to have multiple modes of engagement (visual, auditory, and haptic) so the user has the ability to pick what suits them best at a given moment.

- Another dimension of interoperability comes from assistive technologies working predictably with different combinations of browsers, mobile operating systems, and devices.

- Inclusive tools that allow people with disabilities to partake in a creator-driven, remote-first economy will have a huge advantage over their counterparts.

- At some point in our lives, it's highly likely that we will either face a temporary or situational disability or be a caretaker for someone else. We can treat assistive technology as either a checkbox item, or we can treat it as inspiration for the next generation of cutting-edge technology.

Index

A, B

Accessibility Test Framework (ATF), 119
Accessible Canada Act (ACA), 13
Application Programming
Interface (API), 31
Assistive technologies
artificial intelligence application, 74
broader definition, 78
cognitive impairments
animations, 69
authentication method, 72
auto-updating content, 69
credit card payment screen, 71
digestible format, 68
filters and sorting options, 68
focus indicators, 72
instructions/errors, 69–71
interaction, 68
organized/digestible/
consistent, 66–68
payment screens, 70
reCAPTCHA, 72
types, 66
global settings, 76
guidelines, 76
mobility impairment
dexterity limitations, 74
elements, 76
keyboards, 75
motion actuation/pointer focus, 75
screen readers, 77

speech impairment, 73, 74
user feedback screen, 77
user onboarding messaging, 76
visual impairments (*see* Visual
impairments)
Automated testing
advantages, 118
ATF checks, 119
frameworks, 119
GTXiLib toolkit, 120
limitations, 118
scanners, 120–122
start button, 117
virtual device, 122
Automatic Speech Recognition (ASR), 60

C

Communications and Video Accessibility
Act (CVAA), 11

D

Data visualization
audio chart screenshot, 17, 21, 22
audio-haptic charts solution, 18
customization, 19
description, 15, 16
full-screen implementation, 19
line chart representation, 13, 14
prioritization/technical chart, 15
reference chart, 18, 19

141

© Sukriti Chadha 2023
S. Chadha, *Beyond Accessibility Compliance*, https://doi.org/10.1007/978-1-4842-7948-9